MY MONEY AND GOD

MY MONEY AND GOD

Robert J. Hastings

BROADMAN PRESS

Nashville, Tennessee

To MERRILL D. MOORE
whose book
Found Faithful
first quickened my interest
in the larger implications
of stewardship

© 1961 · Broadman Press
Nashville, Tennessee

All rights reserved
International copyright secured
Fourth Printing

422–255

Library of Congress catalog card number: 61–5393
Printed in the United States of America
5.JUL65KSP

PREFACE

Never before in the history of American life has money been as important as it is today. So much of our daily living is concerned with the accumulation and spending of money. This was not true in colonial America when so many homes were self-sufficient. When each family raised most of its own food, made its own clothing, cleared its own land, and even constructed and furnished its own home, money was relatively unimportant.

Today, very few people in America even approach a state of self-sufficiency. Food, clothing, transportation and housing are mass produced. This is the age of specialization. A plumber may install a kitchen sink and not be able to build a kitchen. A farmer may raise tons of wheat but his wife buys bread at the market. An assembly-man may affix ten thousand radiator caps to highly powered automobiles but never so much as build a soap-box racer for his boys.

We are paid in money for the one service we render in our vocation. In turn, we use this money to buy the hundreds of services and goods available on the market today.

Any treatment of stewardship, then, must give rather major attention to money. Not that money is the crux of stewardship, any more than memorizing John 3:16 is the focal point in Bible study. But since stewardship includes total accountability, and since money plays such a large role in our lives, then the Christian's relationship to his finances is deserving of major attention.

Frequently, a study of money as related to stewardship concerns itself primarily with the giving of money through one's church. The reader will immediately see that this study goes much

further—and begins much sooner—than the act of giving on
Sunday morning. The author feels there are six basic steps in
being a good steward of money. These steps are more easily defined in the form of questions:

(1) How do I earn my money?
(2) What is my attitude toward my money?
(3) Why do I give my money?
(4) How do I give my money?
(5) How do I spend my money?
(6) How do I make final disposition of my money?

This book is an effort to show the significance of each question,
and to suggest practical ways whereby one may successfully complete each step. Also included are "how-to-do-it" suggestions for
help in solving the problems of family budgeting and church
finance.

CONTENTS

CHAPTER ONE
I AM ACCOUNTABLE!

> So then every one of us shall give account of
> himself to God (Rom. 14:12).

Isn't it strange
That princes and kings,
And clowns that caper
In sawdust rings,
And common people
Like you and me
Are builders for eternity?

Each is given a bag of tools,
A shapeless mass,
And a book of rules;
And each must make,
Ere life is flown,
A stumbling-block
Or a stepping-stone.

R. L. SHARPE

"Mr. Webster, will you tell me what was the most important thought you ever had?" The place was the Astor House in New York during the administration of President Millard Fillmore. Twenty men, including Daniel Webster, then Secretary of State, were present for a dinner.

Mr. Webster had been unusually quiet, and the question directed at him was intended to draw him into the conversation. He

1

thought quietly for a few moments; then he replied, "The most serious thought that ever occupied my mind was that of my individual responsibility to God." His simple but profound answer, his twenty minute discourse on the subject, and his immediate withdrawal to his hotel room left a hushed impression on his nineteen fellow diners.

Is there a more sobering thought than the fact that every individual is accountable to God? The haunting thought transcending the specter of our secret sins, of our neglected opportunities, or our wasted money is that some day we must account to God! Every man and woman must account to God. Every boy and girl must answer to God. Every Christian and every non-Christian, every saint and every scoundrel; the wealthy and the poor, the cultured and the uncouth, the lettered and the illiterate—all must account to God.

The Christ of judgment and victory, seen by John on Patmos, had "eyes as a flame of fire," signifying omniscience; and from his mouth proceeded "a sharp two-edged sword" (Rev. 1:14,16). Nothing was hidden from his view and no secret escaped his probing sword.

Paul was exactly right when he warned, "So then every one of us shall give account of himself to God" (Rom. 14:12).

The emphasis in Paul's warning was on the word *himself*. One may not excuse himself by condemning others. The faults of others do not justify one's own shortcomings. Every man must answer —and it must be for himself. He must account for every thought, every word, every deed, every penny, every neglected opportunity, every talent, every breath, every look, every step.

Man is totally and entirely and completely and ultimately answerable to his Maker. This is one of life's inevitables. It is not optional or evadable or elective. Accountability comes in the package of life, and everyone who unties the ribbon of this choicest of God's gifts must answer for each item in the package.

If one is honest, diligent, responsible, and dependable, he will not fear but rather welcome the reckoning. But if, like the embezzler, he covers up and misuses and desecrates the gift of life, then he will live in constant fear and jeopardy of the day when his false bookkeeping and sense of values will be discovered and he stands speechless and defenseless before the divine Accountant.

Definitions

Accountability suggests stewardship. One is a steward because he is accountable; and, contrariwise, one is accountable because he is a steward. Unfortunately, many think of stewardship and the giving of money to a religious organization as being synonymous.

Stewardship and giving are similar. But they are not synonymous. Giving is an expression of stewardship, a facet of stewardship, and often a proof of good stewardship, but never is stewardship to be related merely to church finance.

When the first man and the first woman disobeyed God in Eden, the Lord cried after them, "Where art thou?" (Gen. 3:9). And ever since, the cry of the ages from Creator to the creature has been, "Where art thou?" This is man's inescapable question.

The inquiry was not, "Where is your money, or your time, or your interests?" but "Where are *you*?" God is interested in the total man; and no one area of his life can be marked off so as to say, "Here he is a steward, and here he is not." He is a steward of all or steward not at all.

God, who owns the cattle on a thousand hills, is not so poor that he has to make man a steward to insure receiving proper gifts from him. He can get along without man's gifts. But he cannot get along without man. He could have, but in the act of creation he willed to make the extension of his kingdom dependent in part on man. For this reason, man is steward of all and must answer for all.

As W. H. Greever has well said, "Christian stewardship is the *practice* of the Christian religion. It is neither a department of life nor a sphere of activity. It is the conception of life as a whole."

Stewardship is often described as a trusteeship or a partnership. It is recognizing that all of life's gifts come from the hand of God, all are to be used for the glory of God, and all are to be accounted for at the judgment of God.

Stewardship has been compared to building a service station on one's lot in life, wherever that lot may be, and however that lot may be of service to others.

The sacrifice of animals and fowls in Old Testament worship suggested the idea of total consummation. As the flames on the altar consumed the entire sacrifice, so the worshiper was to think of himself as being totally consumed in service.

Christian stewardship is a lifetime disposition of self, and all that self includes, upon the flaming altar of service. The ideal steward can withhold nothing, waste nothing, dissipate nothing, clutch nothing to his breast.

The good steward has recognized "the invasion of his private life by the larger destinies of mankind." As such, he knows there is no room for littleness, pettiness, and apathy. He is partner with the divine, a servant of the immortal. His life is never the same, once he accepts this principle. He is, in attitude, like the backwoods boy with little schooling who had received his questionnaire regarding induction into the armed forces. He labored with it awhile, puzzled by many of the questions. Then he simply wrote across the top, "I'm ready when you are ready."

On one side of the seal of the American Baptist Foreign Mission Society is an ox standing by a plow. On the other side is an altar. Beneath are the words, "Ready for Either."

The good steward is ready to give or to give up, ready for service like the ox or ready for sacrifice at the altar. He does not claim to be his own master nor does he claim to own his life. He is expendable. In every sense, his life has been invaded with the will of God.

How would you like to live in a world, or even a single community, where everyone was a Christian steward? Do you know of any problems that would not be solved?

Is not stewardship of far deeper implications than deciding how much one will place in the offering plate next Sunday?

Accounts to Be Totaled

If man is totally accountable to God, what are some examples? What are some specific areas of one's life for which one will have to account? The following are merely suggestive. The stewardship of material possessions is omitted since the subsequent portion of this study deals with that specific topic.

Our words.—Jesus said, "Every idle word that men shall speak, they shall give account thereof in the day of judgment" (Matt. 12:36). It is estimated that, were his words recorded, every individual talks enough daily to fill an average size book. The stewardship of daily conversation is a tremendous responsibility.

One day when Bobbie Burns was at the height of his popularity he noticed the admiration of a little boy who followed him around. He turned to him and asked, "Walter, what do you want?" The lad answered that some day he, too, would like to be a great writer. Burns laid his hand on the boy's head as he said, "You can be a great writer some day, Walter, and you will be." The boy became Sir Walter Scott; and, he was everlastingly grateful for the man who spoke a word of encouragement in season. "A word fitly spoken is like apples of gold in pictures of silver" (Prov. 25:11).

Our influence.—Aside from the words we speak and the deeds we commit is the unconscious sharing of our influence. This is too vital an area of life to escape the divine accounting.

In 1871 the *New York Herald* sent Henry M. Stanley in search of David Livingstone, long overdue from his third trip into Africa. He found the missionary explorer in Ujiji, Central Africa, and spent four months with him. Stanley went to Africa a confirmed atheist, but Livingstone's influence—his piety, gentleness, and zeal—won him over. Stanley became a Christian, saying, "I was converted by him, although he had not tried to do it." Livingstone was a good steward of his daily influence.

Centuries ago a young monk went on a preaching tour with the famed St. Francis of Assisi. But to the young monk's surprise, St. Francis simply mingled with the people without preaching a single sermon. His explanation, "My child, we were preaching as we walked and talked with people." The stewardship of influence!

Our time.—Time is man's measurement of life. Nowhere else is he more tempted to be profligate than with the months and years of his life.

Quite famous is the answer John Wesley gave the woman who asked, "If you knew the Lord would come tomorrow night, how would you spend the day?" His answer shows that he refused to allow fear or uncertainty to rob him of a proper investment of his time. He replied, "Madam, I would spend it just as I intend to spend it. I would preach tonight at Gloucester, and again tomorrow morning. After that I would ride to Tewkesbury, preach in the afternoon, and meet the Society in the evening. I should then go to Friend Martin's house, as he expects to entertain me. I would converse, pray with the family, retire to my room at ten o'clock, commend myself to my Heavenly Father, and wake up in glory."

Our love.—One is perhaps at his best as a Christian steward when he is sharing his love, for to give of one's love is truly to give of one's self. The widow's mite meant so much because she gave herself, and Sir Launfal found the Holy Grail when he gave of himself, as well as his bread, to the destitute beggar.

Tolstoy tells of a Russian beggar who stretched out his bony fingers to him for money during a great famine. Tolstoy wished to make a gift, but found he had no money in his pocket. Distressed and apologetic, he seized the beggar's hand and said, "Don't be angry with me, brother, I have nothing to give." The beggar's face lightened as he answered, "But you *have* given me something; you called me brother and that is a greater gift than money."

Our vocation.—One's daily work carries tremendous potential for being a good steward. And neither does one have to serve in a church-related vocation (sometimes erroneously called "full-time Christian service") to be an acceptable steward. Whatever one's occupation, he faces divine accounting for the way he does his work. Always the service motive should be uppermost. Only then can one have inner peace and satisfaction.

When Albert Schweitzer was visiting in America, someone asked, "Dr. Schweitzer, have you found happiness in Africa?" His answer was simple. "I have found a place of service; that is enough for anyone." Schweitzer can be described as a good steward of his vocation because he saw in his daily work an opportunity to make a life as well as to make a living; an opportunity to meet the needs of others, as well as provide three meals a day and a roof over his own head.

Our neglected opportunities.—One must finally account to God for his failures as well as his successes. And a very real failure often overlooked is the refusal to try. Life's greatest failures come not to those who start out to succeed and stumble, but to those who are afraid to start out in the first place.

Hating, killing, stealing, and lying are sins. But Jesus taught that uselessness is a sin also. We must account for our uselessness, our idleness, our folded arms of indifference.

What wrong had the fig tree committed? Was it producing poisonous fruit? Had its root system damaged a nearby garden spot? No. It was guilty of uselessness. No fruit appeared on its limbs. It had done no evil but neither had it done good. Jesus cursed it, as an everlasting lesson that "donothingness" in the kingdom of God is subject to divine anathema.

In the story of the Good Samaritan, the priest and the Levite did no physical harm to the victim lying in the ditch. They simply walked on by, minding their own business. They were poor stewards because they did not consider God's business and their business as one and the same.

In the parable of the talents, Jesus used "wicked" and "slothful" in the same sentence to describe the unfaithful servant. The slothful and the idle and the lazy are wicked! We are accountable for our uselessness and wasted opportunities!

Accountability and My Life

When one has accepted the principle of accountability and seeks to fulfil the role of a good steward, what results? Are there any changes in him? Decidedly so.

Accepting the principle of accountability brings significance to one's life. It adds a sense of urgency, of mission, of destiny. It means that the person who has thought of himself as rather insignificant now sees himself as a partner with God. His name may not be in the headlines, but his life now gains purpose and direction. He handles with care each treasure in the package of life.

Each day has new meaning, each thought new potential, each dollar new power, each opportunity new possibilities! Life now gains a new dimension. It has a frontier! Now, all service is meaningful.

Years ago in London a young and skeptical medical student attended a revival being conducted by Dwight L. Moody. His motive in attending was to "see what a Yankee evangelist looks like." Like a trip hammer, the words of the preacher reverberated, "Let God have your life, let God have your life, let God have your life!" The cynical student grasped the meaning of the dedicated life. Thousands now remember him as Sir Wilfred Grenfell, missionary doctor to the neglected people of Labrador.

This is something of what Emerson meant when he advised, "Young man, go attach yourself to some unpopular minority cause." He knew that life should have direction and purpose. He recognized the principle of the stewardship of the total life, as did Arnold Bennett when he said, "The real tragedy is the tragedy of the man who never in his life braces himself for his one supreme effort, who never stretches to his full capacity, never stands up to his full stature."

Although there is much about George Bernard Shaw we do not admire, we do read with profit his claim that the true joy in life is

being used for a purpose recognized by yourself as a mighty one; the being thoroughly worn out before you are thrown on the scrap heap; the being a force of nature instead of being a feverish, selfish little clod of ailments and grievances, complaining that the world will not devote itself to making you happy.

Mary E. Hardy said it in verse:

> I think I heard a raindrop,
> Said an acorn half awake.
> Time I was up and doing,
> For I have an oak to make.

Purpose, direction, meaning, significance,—these are common words in the vocabulary of the Christian steward. Not that he is obsessed with the starry-eyed idealism of an adolescent or the theoretical abstractions of an ivory-tower philosopher. It is simply that he accepts the fact of divine accounting, sees meaning and purpose even in the simple things of life; and quietly accepts God as a senior partner in all he tries to do and say.

Back in 1939, when the Nazis were at the height of their power in Germany, the following poem appeared in a Berlin newspaper. It signified the militant, aggressive desire of dictatorship to conquer the *wills* of men as well as their *bodies*:

> We have captured all the positions
> And on the heights we have planted
> The banners
> Of our revolution.
>
> You had imagined
> That was all
> That we wanted.
>
> We want more.
> We want all!
> Your hearts are our goal,
> It is your souls we want!

We believe that Nazism is dead, but the struggle for men's hearts is still alive. Chief among the isms that vie for the souls of men is that of materialism, whose god is *things*. Materialists boast that *real* happiness is found in sensual pleasure, in gadgets and trinkets, in higher-powered automobiles, in prime rib steaks, and 100-proof Scotch. Over and over materialists cry:

> Your hearts are our goal,
> It is your souls we want!

But listen. There is another who bids for the souls of men. He comes with no trumpet-fare, rules no armies, wields no sword. He is the Nazarene . . . he is Mary's boy . . . the lowly Galilean . . . the carpenter's son . . . he is the lad from Nazareth. But with the authority of Jehovah himself he calls, "If any man will come after me, let him deny himself, and take up his cross, and follow me. For . . . whosoever will lose his life for my sake shall find it" (Matt. 16:24–25).

Yes, long before materialism beat the drums of twentieth-century gadgetry and prosperity, this itinerant street preacher was saying:

> Your heart is my goal,
> It is your soul I want!

But with what far different motives! God does not want to exploit, but to bless us. He does not want to dominate, but to lead. Neither does he want to crush, but to heal; nor to destroy self-respect and human individuality, but to raise a man to his highest potential. We are his children. He is our Father. He wants the best for us. But before he gives us *his* best, we must give him *our* lives.

So the Christian steward—knowing that God wants all he has, and in joyful recognition that he can never be what God intends without such a full surrender—gladly makes all that he has available for kingdom service.

It might be added that whereas all men are stewards in the sense that they face accountability, the difference in a good and a poor steward is the joyful acceptance or surly rejection of the principle of accountability. Robert G. Lee has popularized the story of Toni Jo Henry in his famous sermon, "Payday Someday." Toni Jo, a convicted murderess, was a steward, but she recognized her stewardship too late. A popular night club entertainer, she had been sentenced to die in the death chamber at Lake Charles, Louisiana, for killing a man in a brawl. When she walked the last mile down death row, one of the reporters whispered, "Good luck, Toni." As she approached the electric chair, she paused to look up at the ceiling. Then she whispered, "I knew all along that God ran the show of his universe; and to think I believed I could steal one little act." She accepted accountability, but it was too late. The curtain was about to be rung down on her final act, and her balance was in the red!

Compare her dance-of-death song with the triumphant resignation of that aged missionary and prince of New Testament stewards, the Apostle Paul. Closing his second epistle to Timothy, he testifies, "For I am now ready to be offered, and the time of my departure is at hand. I have fought a good fight, I have finished my course, I have kept the faith: Henceforth there is laid up for me a crown of righteousness, which the Lord, the righteous judge, shall give me at that day: and not to me only, but unto all them also that love his appearing" (2 Tim. 4:6–8).

Accountability and Material Possessions

So far, little has been said about money, or material possessions. This has been purposeful. Before one can understand any segment of stewardship, he must have an appreciation for the whole. Before one could interpret the Declaration of Independence, e.g., he would need some familiarity with English and colonial American history. The Declaration of Independence is not the whole of American history, but American history includes the Declaration of Independence. The use of money, or material possessions, is not stewardship, but stewardship includes the right use of wealth.

From here on, the study narrows to an interpretation of the stewardship of material wealth or money. We turn from the general to the particular. Whereas, we have been using a telescope to scan the entire horizon of stewardship, now we turn to a microscope for detailed study of that segment of stewardship dealing with material wealth. To write on the general concept of stewardship within any one volume would be too ambitious an undertaking. If stewardship is "neither a department of life nor a sphere of activity" but rather "the *practice* of the Christian religion," then a book on any aspect of the Christian life could be defined as stewardship—centered in its broader application.

Although from here on attention is focused on the dollar and cent features of stewardship, at no point should the reader feel that the proper handling of money alone qualifies one as a good steward. One who is a good steward dollar-wise is more often than not a good steward of all "the manifold grace of God" (1 Peter 4:10).

But not necessarily so! Money is not synonymous with stewardship, and the sooner we make material wealth a segment of stewardship rather than its synonym the sooner we approach the true meaning of accountability of all men before God.

Another common error that needs correcting is identifying the stewardship of money with liberality in giving or with tithing. Just as money is one segment of stewardship, giving is one segment of the stewardship of material wealth.

The steward of wealth is accountable for his wealth, from the first penny that enters his hands until the disposition of his estate, following his death. Giving is a phase of this involved process, but only a phase.

It might simplify matters to state simply that God's first concern with a steward is not with the money he places in the offering plate on Sunday morning. There are other factors. *First*, one might well ask, How did the money come into my possession, i.e., how did I earn my money? *Second*, What is my attitude toward money once I earn it? *Third*, Why do I give my money? *Fourth*, How do I give my money? *Fifth*, How do I spend the portion I keep for myself? And *Sixth*, How do I leave my money when I die? These might be considered the six steps in the development of the Christian steward of material possessions.

The next six chapters discuss these steps in the order given above. The closing chapter deals in a general way with problems of church finance in developing Christian stewards of material wealth.

CHAPTER TWO

HOW DO I EARN
MY MONEY?

> Woe unto him that buildeth his house by
> unrighteousness, and his chambers by wrong;
> that useth his neighbour's service without
> wages, and giveth him not for his work (Jer.
> 22:13).

> O Lord, the sin
> Done for the things there's money in.
>   JOHN MASEFIELD

An exchange student from the Orient was attending summer camp
at a Baptist state assembly. When he developed a toothache, a
friend drove him to a dentist in a nearby town. After a quick examination the dentist said, "It is important that we pull that tooth
immediately. Otherwise it is going to continue giving you trouble.
But the first question—and more important right now—is whether
you have the ten dollars it's going to cost you!" Knowing the boy
was a student from another country and likely of limited means,
the dentist wanted to make sure of his fee before relieving the boy's
misery.

An extreme example? Yes, but it did happen. By a queer chain
of circumstances it could have been possible this dentist was at
least a nominal church member who had contributed money to

missions that led indirectly to this boy's conversion. An extreme improbability, but still a possibility. Assuming that he had given to missions, by no stretch of the imagination or interpretation of the Scriptures could this dentist be described as a good steward, regardless of how liberally he had given to missions.

For before any steward places a gift in the offering on Sunday morning, regardless of size, God is interested first in how that money came into the possession of the giver.

Yes, how one earns his money is just as much a distinguishing mark of the faithful steward as how liberally he gives. Often our zeal for building churches and raising budgets causes us to say, "Well, let him give it. The devil has used his money long enough— let the Lord have a chance with it." But nowhere in the Scriptures is it intimated that the Lord's work is dependent on the fast buck, the quick dollar, the dishonest greenback.

When David approached Araunah the Jebusite to purchase oxen, threshing instruments, and wood for an offering, Araunah offered to *give* them to him. But David refused, "Nay; but I will surely buy it of thee at a price: neither will I offer burnt offerings unto the Lord my God of that which doth cost me nothing. So David bought the threshingfloor and the oxen for fifty shekels of silver" (2 Sam. 24:24). David knew he could not make a real offering unless the ingredients of the offering represented honest toil on his part.

When Ananias made an offering to the Jerusalem church, his reward was instantaneous death. His offering was rejected not because there was any question about the ethics involved in the sale of his property, but that he lied about the amount he received. The transaction was not shady, but the report of it was. This disqualified his gift and brought about his untimely death.

Let it be repeated in every stewardship sermon. Let it be printed in every stewardship tract. Let it be told in every steward-ship study. *God is not interested in the dollar at any cost! His work is not dependent on money from unethical sources! He is just as concerned about how the money gets into a man's wallet as he is in the amount that goes from his wallet into the offering plate!*

The stewardship of material wealth begins, not with the check deposited in the offering Sunday morning, but how the pay check was earned by the giver the previous week.

Work Is Expected

Since it is God's plan for man to work for a living, it logically follows that it is his plan for man to make money. If our economy were purely agricultural and each family thus self-sufficient, there might be some basis for saying that making money is an optional feature for those who have the time and interest to pursue it. But since money is the medium of exchange whereby one barters for most of the necessities of life, then the earning of money is not to be viewed with suspicion or distrust but as the will of God. There is no doubt that every able-bodied man is expected to earn money sufficient for his own needs and those of his dependents. This God expects. But the matter of the amount of money and how one earns it are other questions.

God said to Adam, "In the sweat of thy face shalt thou eat bread, till thou return unto the ground" (Gen. 3:19). And when he instructed that one day in seven should be observed for rest and worship, he also commanded, "Six days shalt thou labour, and do all thy work" (Ex. 20:9). Work during the week is as much the will of God as worship on Sunday. The taint that some associate with making money is not in the fact of earning it but in the manner in which it is earned, as we shall subsequently see.

One of the best known proverbs advises, "Go to the ant, thou sluggard; consider her ways, and be wise: Which having no guide, overseer, or ruler, provideth her meat in the summer, and gathereth her food in the harvest" (Prov. 6:6–8).

And Paul repeatedly emphasized the value and dignity of work:

Let him that stole steal no more: but rather let him labour, working with his hands (Eph. 4:28).
. . . this we commanded you, that if any would not work, neither should he eat (2 Thess. 3:10).
But if any provide not . . . for those of his own house, he hath denied the faith, and is worse than an infidel (1 Tim. 5:8).

There is universal recognition of the value, dignity, and obligation of work. The unfortunate few who do not have to work for a living remind one of the old proverb that "endowed cats catch no mice." Much of the joy and zest of living is missed by those who do not have to earn their own way. For example, there is the compensation of a job well done, of a sense of achievement, that comes to the laborer in addition to the monetary return. When editor William Allen White of Emporia, Kansas, was making a presentation of fifty acres of land for a public park, he said,

This is the last kick in a fistful of dollars that I am giving away today. I have always tried to teach that there are three kicks in every dollar; one when you make it, another when you save it, and the third when you give it.

Those who have made lasting contributions to humanity testify alike of the significance of work. Jesus said, "My Father worketh hitherto, and I work" (John 5:17) and "I must work the works of him that sent me, while it is day: the night cometh, when no man can work" (John 9:4). Jesus taught, in the parable of the talents, the value of using and investing life's blessings. Only the fearful steward who hid his talent in the earth was condemned. The others were praised—regardless of the yield—so long as they kept busy, *using* and investing what had been entrusted to them.

Thomas A. Edison's wife repeatedly urged him to take a vacation. One day he agreed, "All right, but where?" His wife replied, "Decide where you would rather be than anywhere else on earth, and go there." "Very well," he replied, "I will go tomorrow." The next morning he faithfully kept his promise. He went back to work in his laboratory! We are not to conclude from this that vacations are a waste of time. We are to conclude that there is very little real happiness in life outside of a sense of accomplishment, of doing something worthwhile. Work is man's normal condition. God ordained it so in the Garden of Eden, the "birthplace of industry." And only when we perceive that all honest work has the halo of heaven around it will we be able to give ourselves ungrudgingly to it.

Charles Kingsley advised, "Thank God every morning when you get up that you have something to do that day which must be done whether you like it or not!" Dr. Charles Mayo hung on his office wall the motto, "There is no fun like work." And wisely did the preacher observe from life about him that "The sleep of a labouring man is sweet, whether he eat little or much" (Eccl. 5:12). Equally unfortunate, we conclude, are those who work without living and those who live without working!

John James Audubon is an example of one who paid the price of persistence and hard work for near-perfection in his profession. On one occasion he apologized for a very slight defect in his famous painting of a mockingbird being attacked by a snake. He regretted that the defect was a result of having to stop work after only sixteen uninterrupted hours—and that during very hot weather in Louisiana where the painting was done.

Therapeutic Value of Work

Whether or not there is a need for one to earn a living, there is still such constructive value in work that no one should be denied the privilege of working. The unhappy people are those who are consuming much and producing nothing. We eagerly anticipate holidays and vacations. Healthy-minded persons also welcome the return to work and routine. Often the patient who wishes his doctor to prescribe a rest cure needs more than anything else a work cure!

A study was made of 402 persons aged ninety-five years and older. An effort was made to discover the cause of their longevity and to note any characteristics common to all of them. This one common trait was found: the ability to go about one's daily work without tension, worry, and anxiety. Work—within the limits of one's physical stamina—is never harmful. It is only the worry and tension that wears one down. One of the oldsters studied was 106 years of age. He had had a leg amputated when he was 102. Three prosthetic suppliers refused to fit him with an artificial limb, saying it would be a waste of money. In describing how he recovered, the oldster said, "They told me to get a wheelchair, and I told them to go to hell. I learned to walk the first time a hundred years ago, and I could learn again." And he did!

One wonders how many hospital beds and wheelchairs such an attitude would empty, or how many relief and charity rolls it would shorten.

One thinks of Fanny J. Crosby, the prolific hymn writer stricken with blindness as a six-week-old baby. Instead of accepting invalidism and charity, she sought an education and a means of self-support. The philosophy behind her success is shared through these lines, written when she was eight years of age:

> O what a happy soul am I!
>   Although I cannot see,
> I am resolved that in this world
>   Contented I will be;
> How many blessings I enjoy
>   That other people don't!
> To weep and sigh because I'm blind,
>   I cannot, and I won't.
>
>   FANNY CROSBY

Rightly conceived, then, the very fact of work becomes a gleaming facet in the largest meaning of stewardship. One could hardly conceive of a Christian steward spending his days in idleness. There is no justifiable answer to the Master's searching question, "Why stand ye here all the day idle?" (Matt. 20:6).

And before we leave the topic of work, let a word be said for the significance of all honorable toil. Actually, the classification of workers as "white collar," "blue collar," "manual laborers," and so on, is all rather artificial. The man in a ditch whose hands are sticky with muck and mire is doing work no less honorable than the highly-trained surgeon whose hands are anesthetically clean. The quality of one's work is more important than the nature of one's employment. Never are we to look down upon the service rendered by any person, so long as his work is honorable. Never are we to disparage the person who is paid less then we, or whose work requires less training and skill.

The worker sanctifies whatever he is doing by his attitude and integrity. Well did Martin Luther note that "the cobbler who repairs the sole of the Pope's shoe is doing a work as important as that of the Pope who saves the soul of the cobbler." While we do not agree with his theology, we do agree with his analogy. The same ideal echoes from this epitaph on a tombstone in an English churchyard:

> Here lies the body of Thomas Cobb,
> Who made shoes to the glory of God
> in this village for fifty years.

We enjoy laughing at Tom Sawyer's ability to get others to do his work of whitewashing the fence. And we sometimes give mental assent to the proverb, "Don't do anything yourself which you can get others to do for you." There is a certain amount of truth in this piece of advice. But if carried too far, it makes a mockery of the satisfaction that comes from good hard work. It unnecessarily and unjustifiably glorifies the panhandler, the buck-passer, and the sponger.

A housewife says, "When I am blue or discouraged, I start working. The floor may not need scrubbing and waxing, but I clean it anyway. Soon my tensions are gone. Work is good for me."

When Jesus was talking to his disciples about the hereafter, he reminded them that he was going "to prepare a place for you" (John 14:2). This suggests the idea of purposeful activity and work in eternity, in contrast with the somewhat sentimental idea that heaven is a state of continual rest and idleness, a sort of oasis of semi-consciousness! Rudyard Kipling sounds the Christian note when he says that we shall "work for an age at a sitting, and never be tired at all!"

Faith Is Not Excluded

To say that man must earn his living is not to encourage him to neglect dependence on God. An individual can work hard, and still exercise faith in God for daily strength and wisdom to do his work well. Jesus taught, "Seek ye first the kingdom of God, and his righteousness; and all these things shall be added unto you" (Matt. 6:33). The idea here is that right living and faith in God are just as essential in making money as sinew and muscle. Faith and works is the irresistible combination of success in the gaining of material wealth, just as it is in any other endeavor in life.

Again, to say that God expects man to work does not mean that he wants him to work *and* worry. The element of faith will eliminate worry. Jesus warned, "Take no thought for your life, what ye shall eat, or what ye shall drink" (Matt. 6:25). Jesus condemns fretful anxiety that causes one to toss restlessly on his bed at night when he should be soundly sleeping so that tomorrow he will have strength of body for his daily tasks. However, one is not to carry Jesus' warning against worry so far as to justify the fellow with the "devil-may-care" attitude who expects the Lord to feed and clothe his children, pay his rent, give him cigarette money, and bury him when he is dead! Neither is *he* a good steward, nor the man who works himself into a bundle of nerves, worrying if he will have enough to live on.

Furthermore, to say that God demands work from men is not to say one is to claim undue credit for his accomplishments. He is not to boast "I know where *my* money comes from—I work for every penny of it" or "No one ever helped me—I'm self-made!" God warned the Israelites against this attitude as they were about to cross into the Promised Land. He insisted that after they were settled in their homes, surrounded with herds and flocks, well-fed and prosperous, that they were not to "forget the Lord thy God, which brought thee forth out of the land of Egypt" (Deut. 8:14). Regardless of the difficulty in anyone's lot in life, there are always the unearned blessings, including life itself, as well as sunshine and air, friends and loved ones, God's love and care, to mention only a few.

> Back of the loaf is the snowy flour
>   And back of the flour is the mill;
> And back of the mill is the wheat and the shower,
>   And the sun and the Father's will.
>
> MALTBIE BABCOCK

Pay Check Not the First Motive

Another misconception of the responsibility of man to make money is feeling that money is the first objective, that it takes precedence over any other effort in life. "Man, I don't have time to go to church. I have to make a living for my family." Does that sound familiar? It is the cry of one lost in the mad rush for things, one who feels that the main goal in life is to have three meals a day, enough clothes to keep warm, a roof over his head, and a place to sleep at night. Now these are very real necessities, as anyone will testify who long has to go without them.

But are they first? Is one a good steward of material possessions if he thinks the chief aim in life is to make a living? James Truslow Adams recognized the danger of misplaced motives when he said, "There are obviously two educations. One should teach us how to make a living, and the other how to live." It is more than a play on words to say that one should live while he is living. Drawing a pay check at the end of each week will help to keep one alive; it will not insure that he will live!

One's work should bring an inner joy and satisfaction in addition to the monetary return. This is what Margaret Mead meant when she said, "A career is something you would pay others to let you do if they didn't pay you." That is living while you live!

Two wounded veterans occupied adjoining beds in a New York hospital following World War II. Their wounds were almost identical, but their attitudes were poles apart. One talked constantly about how he would take it easy the rest of his life on a government pension. The other studied ways he could make a gainful living in spite of his physical handicap. Which was the better steward?

At least two dangers face the person who considers money-making the chief aim in life. The first danger is the temptation to yield to any method to get wealth. Second, the disappointment and feeling of emptiness that life gives to the man whose god is the making of money.

Look at the first danger. If getting money is so important, then is not any method of earning it justified? This philosophy is summarized in a certain father's advice to his boy: "Son, make money. If you can, make money honestly. But if you can't make money honestly, my son, I still want you to make money!" Such a person's entire moral standard is based on the "so-called" eleventh commandment, "Thou shalt not get caught." He is related to the Dives family, whom Margaret Applegarth describes as "pleasant, prominent, and prosperous" as they sit in their pews with "little dollar signs in their eyes."

It was during the Japanese aggression in China, before World War II. A missionary and a businessman, old friends, were talking. The businessman had had previous business dealings with the Chinese, and was now selling fuel oil to the Japanese. The missionary asked him, "How is it that you spent most of your life with the Chinese, winning their friendship for business reasons, and now you are selling oil to a nation which is dropping bombs on their women and children?" The businessman's answer betrayed his desire to make money at any cost. "Jim, you know how it is. We'd do business with the devil himself if he paid in cash."

The second danger is the loss that comes both to the man and society when money-making becomes the chief end of life. One of the most profound statements Jesus made is found in Matthew 10:39, "He that findeth his life shall lose it." The man who thinks he has it made, who measures achievement by the size of his savings, and who thinks he has life in a corner where he can manipulate it and do with it as he pleases, will find life slipping through his fingers like ashes of roses! "For what shall it profit a man, if he shall gain the whole world, and lose his own soul" (Mark 8:36)?

Judas had ambitious dreams about how he would spend the thirty pieces of silver "earned" by betraying the Lord. But he discovered those silver nuggets had lost all value to him. They were blood stained and ill-gotten. He thought money was the end *of* life only to find that an undue emphasis on riches brings an end *to* life.

In "The Deserted Village," Oliver Goldsmith warned of the danger to society as a whole that comes from an undue emphasis on money-getting:

Ill fares the land, to hastening ills a prey,
Where wealth accumulates, and men decay;
Princes and lords may flourish, or may fade;
A breath can make them, as a breath has made;
But a bold peasantry, their country's pride
When once destroyed, can never be supplied.

Unethical Practices

The ambition to get money at any price results in all types of unethical practices in business, labor, government, management, and the professions. If one sincerely desires to be a good steward of material possessions, he will be aware of and guard against these practices. First and foremost, he will eradicate from his thinking the obsession that money is the chief end in life. He will follow this with practical steps to eliminate unfair or dishonest practices in his daily effort to earn a living.

This means the conscientious steward should seek God's will in the initial choice of a vocation. He will ask first of each possible vocation, Is it legal? It would be preposterous to think that a gambler, a trafficker in narcotics or sex exploitation, or a gangster could be a good steward. His is blood money, tainted with the broken lives of his victims. No serious-minded person would even entertain the thought that one could earn a living by such means and lay claim to Christian stewardship.

Second, he will ask, Is this proposed vocation an honorable one? By "honorable" is not meant "white collar" or any other superfluous or artificial classification of employment. All decent work is honorable, whether one wears a blue, brown, or white shirt. The conscientious construction worker who soils his hand in the murky mire of a sewer is just as honorable as the ethical surgeon whose hands are stained crimson with blood.

By "honorable" is meant whether or not what one is engaged in contributes to the well-being of society. Some jobs are legal but not honorable. The product or service rendered hurts instead of helps. One thinks of the producers of pornographic art, dealers in alcoholic beverages, writers of illicit books and plays, and promoters of legalized racing and related sporting events where gambling, gangsterism, Lord's Day desecration, and related features are the major by-products.

Granted one enters a profession that is both legal and honorable. There is still one more question, and it is the most vital of all, Am I serving in this vocation honestly? That question is significant because it is entirely possible for one to be dishonest and unfair in an honorable profession or vocation. Behind the mask of respectability and legality one can operate in a dishonorable fashion. This is true both for employer and employee, the professional man or the day laborer.

Let it be remembered that money earned dishonestly in an honest profession disqualifies one as a good steward as quickly as "honest" money earned in a dishonorable vocation. It is not so much the title or classification of one's employment as it is the manner in which he carries out his work.

The conscientious man or woman who is seeking to pass acceptably the first test of stewardship—How do I earn my money?—will do well to consider the following questions.

Is it the first aim of an employer to *exploit* his employees, or to use his business as an opportunity whereby both he and those who work for him can *earn* a living?

Are people impersonal "things" to be pushed around for the convenience and at the whim of those in positions of authority? Is man a pack-animal, a blind brute, a mass of muscle available to the highest bidder? Did not Jesus teach that man is better than a sheep (Matt. 12:12)? If so, did he not mean that man was deserving of better consideration than being expected to accept orders blindly and without reason, simply because someone else signs the checks?

Can a Christian steward profit from indecent, firetrap, disease-breeding rental property? What about the civic-minded leaders in a large city a generation ago who discovered that the church to which some of them belonged held title to property in the worst tenement section, where exorbitant rents were charged for quarters unfit for animals to inhabit?

What about merchants who take the attitude of *caveat emptor,*

"Let the buyer beware"? Is it right to take advantage of the ignorance or unsuspecting attitude of the buyer?

Is the good steward proud to have the reputation of being a shrewd operator, an individual who knows how to drive a hard bargain? It is against the law of man to stick a gun in a man's ribs in a dark alley at midnight and take his purse. It is not necessarily against the law of man for a salesman to take advantage of the ignorance of a customer in a business transaction, but is it not against the law of God? Is it not against divine law to misrepresent the value of an automobile or a piece of real estate just so one can have steak on his table instead of hamburger?

Can't make a living otherwise? Would it not be better to earn less, and earn it decently? Would it not be better to lower one's standard of living, if necessary, in order to raise the standard of living of one's brother? Oh, you are not interested in all that dreamy-eyed talk about brotherhood? Are you really interested, then, in stewardship, or just fooling yourself?

> Oh, if we draw a circle premature,
>   Heedless of far gain
> Greedy for quick returns of profit, sure
>   Bad is our bargain!
>   ROBERT BROWNING

Henry B. Trimble gives credence to this viewpoint in *The Christian Motive and Method in Stewardship*:

As civilization becomes more advanced, *possession by intellectual conquest tends to take the place of acquisition by means of physical force.* . . . Under such conditions men have attempted to outwit each other for possession. 'Let the buyer beware' is a principle of English law that illustrates this point perfectly. If a merchant can convince a customer that an article is worth more than its real value, the fault lies with the buyer. But the ethical basis of such acquisition is precisely the same as in the case of the savage taking possession of the hunting ground because he can wield a club with more effectiveness than his competitors.[1]

What about employers who hire workers at the cheapest possible price with no regard whatsoever for human need; or who tolerate unsafe, unsanitary, and undesirable working conditions; or who discriminate against prospective employees for political, racial, social, or religious reasons? Is God pleased with the offerings of money earned under such circumstances? At no point are the Scriptures clearer than the condemnation of such practices in James 5:1–4:

Go to now, ye rich men, weep and howl for your miseries that shall come upon you. Your riches are corrupted, . . . Your gold and silver is cankered; . . . Behold, the hire of the labourers who have reaped down your fields, which is of you kept back by fraud, crieth: and the cries of them which have reaped are entered into the ears of the Lord of sabaoth.

But let it quickly be said that the employer is no more accountable at this point than is the employee. What about the shiftless employee who is a constant clock watcher, who is consistently late for work and takes advantage of lunch periods and other breaks; or who purposefully stages a "slowdown" or is critical of his employer and seeks to undermine his business? Also consider one who creates commotion and discontent among his fellow employees, so that bitterness, dissatisfaction, and suspicion spread like a dark cloud throughout the entire organization? If an employee expects a fair wage, is it not right for his employer to expect a fair day's work in return? One business place posted the following for all the employees to read. It is doubtful if the proprietor had Christian stewardship in mind, but he was not far from the subject.

Loyalty
IF—you work for a man, in heaven's name work for him; speak well of him and stand by the Institution he represents. Remember, an ounce of loyalty is worth a pound of cleverness.

IF—you must growl, condemn, and eternally find fault, why—resign your position and when you are on the outside, damn to your heart's content. But as long as you are a part of the Institution do not condemn it. If you do, the first high wind that comes along will blow you away, and probably you will never know why.

And that is basically what Paul meant in Colossians 3:22–23:

> Servants [employees], obey in all things your masters [employers] according to the flesh; not with eyeservice [clock-watching], as menpleasers; but in singleness of heart, fearing God: And whatsoever ye do, do it heartily, as to the Lord, and not unto men.

What about loan companies that charge exorbitant interest rates, or encourage borrowing and instalment buying beyond the means of the customer? The customer ought to know better? That's good reasoning! It is exactly the attitude Cain took when he tried to justify the first murder, "Am I my brother's keeper?"

A pastor learned that his colored custodian had borrowed $120 which he was trying unsuccessfully to repay. The difficulty was that the contract was so drawn that all his payments were going for interest, so that he could never hope to pay off the loan through regular payments. Other examples could be multiplied, including "hidden costs," "service charges," and like features that prey on the unsuspecting.

What about doctors who profit from malpractice, increasing their incomes through illegal abortions, quack or unnecessary surgery, and illicit traffic in drugs and narcotics; or shyster lawyers, who manage to operate just within the letter of the law but violate the spirit of the law in every case they handle; or corrupt labor leaders who resort to violence, coercion, "gooning," and personal use of union funds?

Think, too, of the firms that will profit from the sale of products which are a hazard to the life and health of the user; or who make dishonest advertising claims, or resort to bribery and unethical lobbying to secure fat government contracts?

Also for consideration is the individual or firm that evades taxes and is always tardy in meeting current obligations, and the person known for the hard bargains he drives (under the guise of "good business head on him"—but where's his heart?) and his constant demand for "discounts" and purchases "at cost"? "At cost" is right—it costs someone! This is not to condemn competition or to

say that one is unchristian if he "shops." Credit for much of our
high standards of living is due to the constant effort to offer a better
product at a lower price. But one can go too far in the direction of
expecting something for nothing, wishing to profit from the mis-
takes and weaknesses of others.

So, in our search for the meaning of the stewardship of material
possessions, we see emerging the word "conscience." *Money-making* must have a conscience if *money-giving* is to be pleasing to
God. And the power of the conscience to rob a man of the pleasure
of ill-gotten wealth is still as real as it was the day Judas slammed
the thirty silver coins on the Temple pavement and went out to
find a rope strong enough to break his neck.

> You'll pay. The knowledge of your acts will
>   weigh
> Heavier on your mind each day,
> The more you climb, the more you gain,
> The more you'll feel the nagging strain.
> Success will cower at the threat
>   of retribution. Fear will fret
> Your peace and bleed you for the debt;
> Conscience collects from every crook
> More than the worth of what he took,
> You only thought you got away
> But in the night you'll pay and pay.
>   ANONYMOUS

Business and Religion Do Mix

A businessman was offered a deal to make a great sum of quick
money. He declined the offer, giving Christian principles as his
reason. His friend countered, "Surely you don't try to mix two
good things like business and religion." He answered, "I have discovered that it is only when we do mix business and religion that
we can *prove* our religion and *improve* our business!"

As a young man, J. C. Penney invested his savings in a butcher
shop. He was advised to buy a bottle of whiskey each week for the
chef of the local hotel, his best customer. He purchased a bottle
the first week, then quit when he became convicted it was wrong.

He lost his business but won his self-respect and later made a fortune in retail selling.

Then there was the Christian fish merchant in Boston many years ago who formed a partnership with some other men to buy up all the codfish brought into their harbor. Then they raised the prices and sat back to wait for a killing. But in a few days the Christian partner broke up the deal. He explained, "When I knelt in prayer at family altar, a whole mountain of codfish rose between me and God as I thought of the poor people who were going hungry. Gentlemen, I would not let all the fish in the Atlantic Ocean come between me and the Lord."

And we are reminded of the old Scot who was pressured by a local committee to sell liquor in his store. They threatened boycott if he refused. He replied, "I want you to know, gentlemen, that my goods are for sale, but not my character."

A man of many business interests in Prichard, Alabama, was converted. One of his holdings was a beer distributorship, which the previous year had netted him $67,000. One of the first things he did was to sell it. He explained, "I cannot claim to be a Christian and have beer trucks driving over town with my name on the sides."

And a lawyer said, "I had to quit serving a particular insurance company because of its demand that I pressure claimants into settling for less than they deserved."

Examples could be multiplied of men who do mix religion and business, who do face the inevitable conclusion that stewardship begins with how the dollar gets into a man's pocketbook, and not with the dollars that go into the collection basket on Sunday. In the face of multiplied temptations to make a quick or unethical dollar, they are determined to honor God first by giving full measure service rendered for every dollar received.

Have you, to your own satisfaction, passed the first test, How do I earn my money? If so, you are ready for the second, "What is my attitude toward money, once I have earned it?"

CHAPTER THREE
WHAT IS MY ATTITUDE TOWARD MY MONEY?

For the love of money is a root of all kinds of evil (1 Tim. 6:10, ASV).

Whate'er thou lovest, man,
    That too become thou must,
God, if thou lovest God,
    Dust, if thou lovest dust.
ANGELUS SILESUS

Money is neither good nor evil. It is neither moral nor immoral. Money is amoral. It is capable of good or evil, depending on the use made of it.

Most things in life are that way. Take as simple an example as water. Water is neither good nor evil. It is neither moral nor immoral. Water is amoral. It is capable of good or evil, depending on the use.

Water can sustain human life, wash away impurities, and nourish vegetation. It can change the desert into a paradise. It can refresh a weary traveler, provide transportation for men and commerce, and delight the heart of carefree youth as they splash in summer and skate in winter.

But water can be evil. Uncontrolled in the form of swiftly rising streams and rivers it can flood great cities and sweep away tons of precious topsoil. Polluted by bacteria, it can spread disease of epidemic proportion through entire communities. Water can snuff out life or sustain it. The same water can kill or enliven. The difference lies in how the water is used, how it is controlled.

Lay a dollar bill before you. Look it over carefully. Read the printing, study the symbols. Analyze it any way you wish, even with a microscope. The only conclusion one can arrive at is that money is a harmless bit of green paper, the benefit or harm arising therefrom depending entirely on the use that is made of it.

The same dollar can print pulp magazines or New Testaments. It can build hospitals or honky-tonks. It can send missionaries or missiles.

Money, rightly used, can make one magnanimous of heart and generous of soul. Wrongly used, it can leave one bitter and selfish and sarcastic. The test of money is the use of money. It can bless or curse, heal or kill, beautify or uglify.

One should, then, study its use as he studies the habits of a deadly cobra or the characteristics of a dangerous explosive. Money deserves our respect without our worship, our mastery over it without our bondage to it.

Use Based on Attitude

Now the use one makes of money is dependent on one's attitude toward money. Attitude will determine if one is liberal, covetous, miserly, profligate, frugal, generous, charitable, parsimonious, prodigal, extravagant, penurious, churlish, mercenary, greedy, or lavish.

This is why the good steward must successfully pass the test of attitude toward wealth before he begins to think about the stewardship of the use of his money. Christian stewardship includes the motive and intent of the heart, as well as the sum written on the face of an offering envelope or the amount one wastes in selfish, indulgent living.

It is most interesting to note that Jesus discussed one's position regarding material wealth far more than he did the use of money. He knew that proper use follows proper attitude. He did not, e.g., outline a detailed plan for financing his kingdom. However, through parable and discourse, Jesus did warn his disciples and would-be followers that love for God must supersede love for money; undue confidence should not be placed in material wealth; the finer values of life are not to be confused with the things that money can buy; money is only of temporary value; and that money is not worth the worry that many people pay for it.

Our search for the Christian attitude toward money leads to a consideration of its meaning or definition. Proper understanding can encourage a Christian attitude; Christian attitude will encourage Christian use.

Wealth Defined

It has been stated already that money is "a harmless bit of green paper, the benefit or harm therefrom depending entirely on the use that is made of it." Money is also defined as "the coinage of one's life." As such, it often, but not always, represents the time, energy, sweat, and toil that goes into the earning of it.

Money is also legal tender; i.e., if one incurs an indebtedness, his creditor is obligated by law to accept recognized currency as just payment.

Money is also a measure or standard of value. The value of an object or service may be judged by the amount of money it costs. Thus, it becomes an acceptable medium of exchange.

A customer wants a certain advertised product. All he has to offer is his time. The merchant does not want the customer's time, but the customer can put in so many hours working for an employer who will pay him a certain number of dollars which may in turn be exchanged for the merchandise. Modern life would be paralyzed without a simple, standardized medium of exchange.

Money has two characteristics that further simplify its definition. First, printed currency or coins have little or no intrinsic value in themselves. True, coins have some value as far as the metal used is concerned. But it is illegal to mar a coin in such a way as to extract any usable or valuable metal. A bill or a coin has only the value that the government and/or public opinion assigns to it. It costs about two-tenths of one cent for paper and ink to print a one dollar bill or a fifty dollar bill. The fifty dollar bill is accepted at greater value because it is a symbol of more products or more service rendered. But the value is intrinsic and symbolical only. Inflation or deflation can quickly change the value of money. It is entirely possible for a one hundred dollar bill to be worth a year from now only as much as a dollar bill is today.

This suggests a second characteristic of money, its corruptibility. If one were seeking a single adjective from the English language that most nearly defines material wealth, it is doubtful if a better one could be found than "corruptible." All the gold which has been mined from the bowels of the earth since men first began to search for it in the land of Havilah to the last bar deposited in Fort Knox has one common characteristic: it is corruptible. Jesus verified this by saying, "Lay not up for yourselves treasures upon earth, where moth and rust doth corrupt, and where thieves break through and steal" (Matt. 6:19).

Our soldiers were evacuating Corregidor during World War II. Everything that might prove of value to the enemy was being destroyed, including neatly stacked bundles of U. S. currency. The tired, battle-weary soldiers watched quietly. One soldier picked up a hundred dollar bill and used it to light a cigarette, saying, "I always wanted to do this." Time was running out on Corregidor, and money had very little meaning. It was corruptible!

Paul Geren in his *Burma Diary* describes a similar situation when refugees were streaming on foot from Burma to India during the early days of World War II. Finding their money of no value, many of them threw it away, recognizing that a given weight of food was more valuable than the same weight in gold. Gold was corruptible!

But someone quickly adds, "I have my wealth invested in property, in priceless art, in precious stone. Its value is secure."

Is it? Who said so? Were the French landowners secure after the French Revolution? Did the Russian nobility save their crowns and jewels and palaces after the Communist-inspired revolution?

Remember that the value of any material object or even one's service depends on the recognition by others of one's right to ownership.

One's property might be condemned in the public interest; it could be confiscated in time of riot or war; its control can be taken from you when you are proven mentally incompetent to manage it.

A deed to a piece of property is good only so long as others recognize your legal claim to own it. When this recognition ceases, there is nothing one can do to maintain it except by force, and superior forces will overwhelm one if the majority of public opinion is against him.

No person owns anything more than others are willing to admit that he owns! And granted others recognize one's right to ownership, the slow, steady, and sure termites of time, disease, old age, and death will strip each person of every vestige of material wealth, so that like Alexander the Great one may as well request his hands to be arranged open in death so that the disbelieving can see that shrouds have no pockets and dead men's hands hold no gold! Yes, money is corruptible!

A Universal Temptation

Granted that money—though corruptible—is necessary, that it performs a valuable service, that it is a worthy incentive for work, there is almost the universal temptation to give to money an intrinsic value that it does not possess. We habitually give it more credit than it is due and place on it a higher valuation than it deserves. It is at this point that one can fail in his attitude toward money, i.e., in deciding whether money shall be one's servant or one's master.

This is the dividing line between the faithful and the unfaithful steward. Here is where one decides the direction and purpose of his life relative to wealth. If he bows to money as a pagan bows to an idol, then his use of money is bound to be unchristian. But if a steward delegates to money the role of a servant, over which he maintains the mastery, then he is more likely to be Christian in his earning, giving, spending, and saving of money.

In 1 Timothy 6:10, Paul placed his finger on the sore spot of the infection of improper attitude toward money. Often misquoted, but never to be neglected, is his famous declaration, "For the love of money is a root of all kinds of evil" (ASV). This is the answer!

To love money is a source or taproot of all kinds of sin. To have money is not a sin. Money is not tainted. Money is neither a devil nor a saint. But the love of money, that's the crux! Negatively stated, this is not the Christian attitude. This is not the position of the faithful steward. He refuses to fall in love with dollars and cents, for out of that love he sees the germinal source of all kinds of wickedness.

What does it mean to love money? To love money is to believe that dollars and cents can unlock any door and buy any privilege. To love money is to put one's checkbook on a pedestal and go to any limit of physical exhaustion or diabolical conniving to increase one's account. To love money means one will resort to unethical and dishonest methods to get it. To love money means one will sacrifice family and individual happiness, peace of mind, and the finer virtues of life to acquire it. To love money means that one believes the possession of it places one in a special category of society that is better and superior to others, giving him the privilege to look down his nose disparagingly at the "less fortunate." To love money is to believe that success is always spelled $ucce$$.

And let no one say that because he is of limited income he is not tempted to love money. A part-time laborer, earning ten dollars a week, can love money just as much as a professional entertainer earning a thousand dollars a week. The love of money is not the pastime of the idle rich. The pauper can have his idol of gold before which he prostrates himself as surely as the playboy millionaire who lives on the earnings of a past generation.

The Dangers of Materialism

Love of money is a deadly cobra because it is the brother of materialism. Ethically speaking, materialism is thinking that economic well-being, "especially of the individual himself, should rule in the determination of conduct."

The money-lover, the materialist, allows this self-made god to become the master of his life. His conduct, his spending habits, his philosophy of life—all revolve around the securing and use of "things." What he can total on an adding machine, deposit in a bank, hold with his hands, taste in his mouth, and see with his eyes become life's ambitions. As such, he rules God out of his life.

The materialist could never hope to be a Christian steward, even though he were a strict tither! Jesus clearly warned "Ye cannot serve God and mammon" (Matt. 6:24b). One might conceivably be a servant of mammon, a materialist, and give liberally for selfish reasons but still be a thousand miles from Christian stewardship!

This is why it is so everlastingly important to link one's attitude and method of earning money to the stewardship of material possessions! Leading people to give is secondary, a by-product. First is one's intent, purpose, direction, and motive. Of secondary and lesser importance is the question of his liberality in giving.

A humorous insight into materialistic philosophy was the story in the small town weekly newspaper describing the robbery and murder of a local businessman. He had been waylaid after work the previous Saturday night on his way home. "But fortunately for the deceased," noted the reporter, "he had just deposited his day's receipts in the bank, with the result that he lost nothing but his life!"

More sobering was the comment made by a middle-aged professional man to one of his close friends. They were spending an afternoon at the country club. The professional man, because of training and experience, should have been at the zenith of his usefulness. His vocation was one of great potential service to society. Yet, he said in noticeable disgust, "You know, I wish I had enough money to tell the rest of the world to go to hell!" Gone was the idea of altruistic service, of meaning and mission of life. Enthroned in his materialistic mind was the god of dollars and the puny things that dollars can buy.

Compare the young man who said, "If I had $100,000 to spend while I'm here on earth, I would be willing to have my soul lie in hell for all eternity after I'm dead." Of course, the young man forgot to note that in hell he would not be dead, but very much alive! But his pitiful plea is evidence of the widespread feeling that any price is worth paying for the luxury of complete submersion in the things of life, even though the enjoyment thereof is temporal and lasts but for a season.

The American craze for the things of life is the theme of a sermon, "Christ's Cure for This Aspirin Age," by Paul L. McKay in the September, 1951 issue of *Pulpit Digest*. The sermon suggests three symbols of contemporary life. All three are rooted in materialism.

Mr. McKay lists the herky-jerky, glittering neon sign as the first symbol. He sees in the brilliant, dancing lights a symbol of the perpetual movement of a people, restless in their search for life's "things."

He sees a second symbol in the can opener, a common household article. The can opener is a symbol of a machine-minded age, which kneels before the shrine of gadgets and convenience.

The aspirin bottle is the third symbol. The millions of pounds of aspirin which Americans consume annually are an indictment of the splitting headaches resulting from a herky-jerky, gadget-conscious type of civilization.

Edward K. Ziegler echoes the same idea in his "Materialist's Version of the Twenty-third Psalm":

> Science is my Shepherd, I shall not want;
> He maketh me to lie down on foam-rubber
>   mattresses;
> He leadeth me beside six-lane highways.
> He rejuvenateth my thyroid glands;
> He leadeth me in the paths of psychoanalysis
>   for peace of mind's sake.
> Yea, though I walk through the valley of the
>   shadow of the iron curtain, I will fear
>   no communist; for thou art with me; thy
>   radar screen and thy hydrogen bomb, they
>   comfort me.
> Thou preparest a banquet before me in the
>   presence of the world's billion hungry
>   people.

Thou anointest my head with home permanents.
My beer-glass foameth over.
Surely prosperity and pleasure shall follow
me all the days of my life; and I will
dwell in Shangri-la forever.

Hidden in as ancient a book as Deuteronomy is a verse as modern as tomorrow in its commentary on contemporary life: "But Jeshurun waxed fat, and kicked: thou art waxen fat, thou art grown thick, thou art covered with fatness; then he forsook God which made him, and lightly esteemed the Rock of his salvation" (Deut. 32:15).

Yes, that's the rub—"he forsook God which made him." Things, in and of themselves, are not evil. The difference in the materialist and the Christian steward is *not* that one lives a life of asceticism, denying himself all but the bare necessities of life while the other fares sumptuously, but that one acknowledges God while the other bows in subjection before the altar of "things."

Dr. Walter Judd, one time medical missionary to the Orient, tells an experience that differentiates the two. When he graduated from medical school, one of his professors chided him for wanting to "waste" his life in medical missions. But when Dr. Judd returned to his alma mater on a furlough, his scoffing professor sought him out for counsel. "You remember, Judd," he began, "how I advised you against going to the Orient? I'm not so sure now. Take my own life for instance. As a young man, I had four major ambitions, all of which have been realized. First, I wanted to be the best possible doctor I was capable of becoming. Second, I wanted to be a doctor's doctor, a man other medical men would seek when they needed attention. You know my achievements, and how these two dreams have been realized.

"Third, I wanted an income so I could have a home with the appointments my family could enjoy, so that my children would rather bring their friends home than take them any place else. Fourth, I wanted a fine wife and children. You know something of my income, of the house where we live, of my lovely wife and two children. But Dr. Judd, I feel as if all these things are slipping through my fingers. What's wrong with my life?"

Dr. Judd says he was kind enough not to speak the truth to his old professor. But in his heart he was saying, "Sir, there is nothing wrong in the four ambitions you set for your life. The only difficulty is that they all revolved around you and your family. You did not go far enough in your dreams, and now you are seeing the truth of Jesus' warning that those who think they can find their lives and order them to their own interests eventually will lose them."

The sin of materialism is its shortsightedness. It sees only self, and food for the next meal and a bed for tonight. Life has no other meaning, no other significance.

Materialism is truly the brother of money-love. They speak the same language and walk hand in hand down the path of life. The result is no room on the path for the selfless One who said, "a man's life consisteth not in the abundance of the things which he possesseth" (Luke 12:15).

Limitations of Money

The disappointing feature about materialism and money-love is that they fail to keep their promises! "Buy this, and your life will be radiantly happy!" "Own this, and you will be the envy of all who know you!" "A new day for your family when you bring it home!"

Ever watch a fly try to free himself from old-fashioned fly paper? When he first makes a three-point landing on the gooey, sweet-smelling stickiness he thinks, "My fly paper!" Here is just what he needs to satisfy his appetite. But watch him as he vainly struggles and hopelessly beats his wings against the air. Listen. The fly paper says, "My fly!"

Listen to Jesus describe the rich fool who said "My corn, my barns!" At last he had $ucce$$ within his grasp. He had life in a corner and he was going to enjoy it for all it was worth. No more worry about crop failures for him! No concern about drought or flood. No anxiety about labor trouble. No disappointment over late rains and early frosts. Man, he had it made. He was financially independent! He, too, could tell the rest of the world "to go to hell."

The unfortunate rich farmer made only one error. (Being a graduate of the state A & M college he should have known better!) He thought a man's soul, like the flesh of a hog, could be fattened on corn! He didn't know a man could die spiritually and go to hell with a barn full of grain. As death slipped her icy fingers about his neck he thought he could hear his barns say, "My fool, my fool!"

Yes, money can do many wonderful things. But its limitations are as great as its potentialities.

Money can buy the finest innerspring mattress, but it cannot assure the sleep of an innocent baby to a troubled mind. Money can buy the choicest foods but fail to satisfy the inner hunger of the soul. It can provide a dream vacation to the exotic corners of the world, but money cannot get a person away from himself.

Money can open doors to the best institutions of higher learning in the land, but it cannot buy "the wisdom that is from above" which "is first pure, then peaceable, gentle, and easy to be intreated" (James 3:17). Money can secure the highest skilled medical help, but it cannot buy even one minute of life. Money is powerful, but not as powerful as some men think.

Wholesome Attitudes

While it is true man cannot serve God *and* mammon, he can serve God *with* mammon. A right attitude toward money is accepting it as a tool, a servant, an aid. There is no evil in money or the things money can buy. God wants us to have the "things" of life— in fact, he promised that if one would seek his kingdom first then he would find the necessary "things" added to his life (Matt. 6:33).

How can one be sure he has the right attitude toward money? How can he be sure of relegating wealth to the role of servant rather than master? Three tests are suggested.

First, Can one find joy in life experiences though denied material comforts? Or stated differently, Does an easy life insure happiness?

A wonderful testimony on this subject was given at the ground-breaking ceremonies for the Truett-Scarborough-Fleming memorial building on the campus of Southwestern Baptist Theological Seminary in 1946. Mrs. L. R. Scarborough, widow of one of the former presidents for whom the building was to be named, was asked to speak briefly. She reminisced about the difficult days during the depression years when new buildings and expansion were impossible. She commented on the postwar prosperity and her joy in seeing the new construction. Then she closed, "But as I look back over my life, I cannot help but say that those difficult, debt-ridden depression years produced the happiest experiences of my life." Was she decrying the new prosperity and growth of the seminary? No, she did not intend that. She was simply saying that economic security, comfort, and convenience are not prerequisites for happiness. Dollars do not equate joy!

A second test of one's attitude toward wealth, Does he prize money so greatly that he is willing to hazard the life and health of himself or his family to secure it? Does he sacrifice the happiness of his loved ones in a mad, frightening rush to make every possible dollar?

An extreme example, but universal and basic in its application, is an experience related to the writer by an elderly lady in southern Illinois. She said, "Many years ago when I was a young girl, a rabid dog in our rural community bit a young man and me. Back then, serum for the treatment of rabies was not locally available. So the owner offered to pay our full expenses to Chicago for the inoculations, or five hundred dollars in cash. I boarded the Illinois Central for Chicago and stayed the time necessary for adequate treatment. In the 1890's, five hundred dollars looked like a fortune. So the young man said he would prefer the cash, and assume the risk of not securing medical aid. When I returned home, the unfortunate boy was dead and buried."

An extreme example? Yes. But how many men and women lie in premature graves because they drove themselves mercilessly or took unnecessary risks to make that last dollar? And how many who are still living might as well be dead as far as any satisfaction they are getting out of life or any source of joy they are to their families is concerned, for they have been bitten by the dog of ambition whose saliva is teeming with the bacteria of greed.

The last test, Has one's dependence on money erased his dependence on God? Does he fear that the only help available is the help from a regular income? Has he eliminated God? Has he forgotten the meaning of childlike trust?

An example comes again from the writer's experience. It was my privilege for five years to be the pastor of a retired schoolteacher who had an enviable record of faithfulness to her church through her talents of time, influence, and money. Her twenty-five year record of teaching the third grade in public schools was almost matched by her service in teaching Intermediate girls in Sunday school. Nothing was too good for her church, her pastor, her friends.

But the way had not been easy. Left a young widow with four small children, she entered a university to qualify for teaching so as to support her dependent family. There was financial struggle, but God always came first. One day her insurance man called, "Mrs. Hall, the premium on your house insurance is about due." Other bills were pressing. Something had to go unpaid, and it was the insurance.

Soon after, as she was walking home from her third grade classroom, she noticed a fire truck and people gathered in the street near her home. She wondered whose house was afire. Her fears were justified, for it was her own. Doubly bad, her insurance had expired. She stood helplessly on the sidewalk watching the damage of smoke, fire, and water, as her furniture was dragged into the streets.

Before long her agent, attracted by the fire in the small town, drove up. He said quietly, "Mrs. Hall, do not worry about your home. Although it is against the recommendations of my company, I paid your premium the other day. Your insurance is in force. You will be paid for your loss."

This dear lady did not have such experiences every day, neither was her habit of life one of presumption on the mercy of God. But she had had enough like experiences to cause me to ask, "Mrs. Hall, what has been the secret of your quiet faith through the years?" She did not hesitate a minute as she replied, "I have never allowed the dollar bill to get bigger than my God!"

I have never allowed the dollar bill to get bigger than my God!

Did you ever hear a better stewardship testimony, a more effective ten second sermon? In thirteen simple words she summarized all that this chapter has tried to say. Her testimony captures the spirit of this entire discussion on one's attitude toward money.

Now we are ready for step three in our pursuit of the stewardship of material possessions. Have you passed steps one and two? Are you Christian in the manner you earn your money? Are you Christian in your attitude toward money, once you earn it? Then you are ready for test three, Why do I give my money?

CHAPTER FOUR
WHY DO I GIVE MY MONEY?

> *Remember the words of the Lord Jesus, how he said, It is more blessed to give than to receive (Acts 20:35).*

> Love ever gives—
>   Forgives—outlives—
> And ever stands
>   With open hands.
> And, while it lives—
>   It gives.
> For this is Love's prerogative,—
>   To give,—and give,—and give.[1]
>   JOHN OXENHAM

"It is more blessed to give than to receive." Jesus was always making such extreme statements. There was an extravagance about his messages that must have rudely awakened the nominal listener. His teachings were so different from popular conceptions. What he said so often ran counter to "common sense." Note some examples.

The world says that happiness comes by satisfying every personal desire, while Jesus taught that those who find their lives will lose them (Mark 8:35). The world teaches that greatness comes through the office or position one holds, while Jesus remarked that true greatness comes through service rendered, regardless of the of-

44

fice (Mark 10:44). The world says that success awaits the ambitious
go-getter, while Jesus taught that the meek, the teachable, the lead-
able will inherit the earth (Matt. 5:5).

The world says to return the kindness of friends, but Jesus said to
love one's enemies as well (Matt. 5:44). The world says that the
kingdom of God is identified with adult leadership and character-
ized by institutions and buildings and organizations, but Jesus
taught that the kingdom is like the humility of a child (Luke 18:16)
and that its truest expression is in one's heart (John 18:36).

Just as disturbing is his interpretation of giving. The world mag-
nifies the pleasure that comes from earning, from getting, from receiving. But Jesus, true to form, said, "It is more blessed to give
than to receive" (Acts 20:35). One can be happier in giving than
getting, in sharing than earning, in disbursing than receiving. And
if we have not found this true in our experience, it is not so much a
refutation of the truth of Jesus' message as it is a confession of our
immaturity in Christian stewardship.

More joy in giving than getting! More satisfaction in sharing
than receiving! How strange are these words. How foreign-sounding
to these twentieth-century ears of ours. How contrary to popular
advertising.

Were these words meant only for the simple peasant life of the
first-century believers, sheltered as they were from much of our
modern-day competition, high standard of living, technological
know-how, and material comforts? Or is there still more joy in giving than in acquiring?

Like any other verse in the Bible, Acts 20:35 must be interpreted
in the light of its context, in the framework of the total Scriptures.
And this involves such topics as the sequence *in* giving, the motives
for giving, and the amount *of* one's giving. "Man looketh on the
outward appearance, but the Lord looketh on the heart."

The how of one's giving is perhaps more closely related to the
blessings of giving than is the fact of giving. This is true in all areas
of the Christian life. Not what we say, but how we say it. Not to
whom we witness, but how we witness. Not when we go to church,
but how we go. Not the fact we give, but how we give.

The Right Sequence in Giving

We have said that why one gives his money is the third test of the stewardship of material possessions. So many feel that stewardship begins and ends when the collection plate is passed on Sunday morning.

But actually one is not ready for this step until he has successfully passed tests one and two. First, How do I earn my money? Second, What is my attitude toward money? If these two questions are not answered satisfactorily, then one would do violence to the Scriptures to claim the blessings of Acts 20:35 on his giving. If one has been dishonest and unscrupulous in earning his money, if he is materialistic in his attitude, there could be little joy when he comes to the act of giving, all of which suggests the importance of sequence in giving.

As vital as giving is, other matters come first. And unless they do come first, the giver had just as well keep his money for himself. Paul mentions sequence in his description of the churches in Macedonia. Although the members were poverty-stricken, their offerings had been most generous. His explanation: "they . . . first gave their own selves to the Lord" (2 Cor. 8:5).

They first gave themselves! This placed giving in the right sequence! Self preceded substance! Truly, this is one of the mountainpeak stewardship verses of the Bible.

In her unique book, *Twelve Baskets Full*, Margaret T. Applegarth shares the story of a missionary in Africa to show how self must precede substance.

The missionary had requested from her home church early in the summer such items as pencil stubs, colored thread, flower seeds, and so on, for the natives at Christmas. The box was late in coming. The native children grew restless and daily asked the white Mamma if they should pray for a big wind to hurry the boat. When it finally arrived, all it contained was a mass of hard, melted Christmas candy. The humidity and the long trip had made of the sweets one gummy mess.

What to do? Throw it away? Write a stinging letter to the

thoughtless women at home who had found the easiest way out to send a gift? Perhaps, except for one factor—the missionary had first given her life. So she added to her gift of self the gift of substance, the candy.

Initiative and resourcefulness came into play. She heated and melted the candy again, forming beautiful patterns with the multicolored flavors.

Two hundred natives were invited to the Christmas party, each having been asked to bring a large leaf. A line was formed. She dipped one spoon of melted candy onto each leaf, quoting each time, "O taste and see that the Lord is good." Simple? Yes. But wait. A few months later the missionary was visiting an old chieftain. She noted a withered leaf in a jar. He explained that each month when the moon was full he opened the jar to lick the leaf. Each time he remembered how lovely Christmas was!

Christmas was lovely, and the candy was lovely, and Christ was made lovely, because the gift of self had preceded the gift of substance. In the depths of the dark continent, a lonely (or was she lonely?) missionary placed giving in the right sequence.

The Right Motive in Giving

Closely related to sequence in giving is the motive that prompts one to give. Why *do* people give?

Motives for giving are many. One person will give for one reason, while another is prompted by an entirely different motive. Some motives are good; some are not so good. Some are Christian; some are not. The blessings one receives, or fails to receive, are closely related to one's motives.

One should constantly re-evaluate his motives. If he finds his motives are wrong, he should remedy the error. Some people seem to step up in their motives over a period of years. A baser motive may prompt their first efforts at giving, but as they become enlightened and informed there is a transition in their motivation. This study may help you in discovering a higher motive for your giving, and hence open the doors to greater blessings.

The following discussion of motives is not presented as exhaustive. The various shadings and overlapping of motives may be as numerous as there are givers. But it is felt the list is representative. The reader, through self-examination, may be able to detect other motives than these in his own life.

Self-analysis of one's motivation is always a helpful experience, particularly if self-improvement results. The conscientious steward must not be afraid to lay bare his own heart and soul if he wants to progress in Christian stewardship. He must be as critical, and more, as the doctor who probes for a hidden malady that will sap one's vitality unless remedied.

Are you ready? Are you willing to examine your own motives? Then begin with

The motive of fear.—Fear, rightly controlled, is an asset. Fear makes one look in both directions before crossing a street. Fear helps one to obey the rules of health so as to guard against illness and postpone death. Fear can be of value in the Christian life. "The fear of the Lord is the beginning of wisdom" (Prov. 9:10). It can lead one to obey the commandments, respect the word and will of God, and to lead a life of humility and dependence on the Lord.

But fear can be a liability. It can paralyze. It can make one overly cautious. It can make one retreat when he should advance. Fear caused the unfaithful steward to bury his talent in the earth, rather than investing it. If one thinks of God as a policeman with a big stick constantly on the lookout for some misdemeanor, then his conception of God is wrong. If one brings his offerings like a cringing, fear-ridden animal, then he is guided by a poor motive.

There are those who, in fear, look upon God as a bill collector. This type of personal testimony is not at all uncommon:

Giving to the church is like paying my fire insurance—I couldn't go to sleep at night otherwise. There are so many uncertainties in life, so many things that could happen. I remember an evangelist one time who described a family who stopped tithing for just one week. The next Friday they had a wreck that cost them ten times what their tithe would have been. This preacher stated that God is a good collector— if he doesn't get our offerings willingly, he can get them through doctor bills and things like that.

When this type of individual gives, he imagines that God is looking over his shoulder, in the form of a combination policeman and
collector. Would you say he is a good steward, regardless of his liberality?

The error in this type of reasoning is in thinking that the Christian can avoid evil in this world if he can just get God on his side!
So he attempts to win God over, sometimes by agonizing prayer
that seeks to change the mind of God, and sometimes with gifts of
money.

But is one justified in thinking he can buy the favor of God? Are
happiness, prosperity, and health always signs of godliness? Are
there no values in illness, sorrow, and suffering? This is the eternal
problem answered by the book of Job, and the answer was that a
good man can suffer and be godly at the same time. One could be
very liberal and still suffer many afflictions. Contrariwise, he might
be very selfish and yet be relatively free from afflictive or adverse
conditions.

A man faced the choice of taking one of two trains to a particular
destination. The routing of the two was only slightly different.
When he learned later that the train he had chosen not to ride had
had a disastrous wreck, he cried, "What a wonderful Providence!"
But a nearby friend commented, "What about the people on the
other train?" This is not to deny the fact of God's providential care
of his people. It is to deny that the expressions of providence are
always convenient.

Charles T. Holman notes, with keen insight, "Religious persons
are not exempt from the rule of law. . . . Pneumonia and careen-
ing cars take their toll alike of the religious and the irreligious. . . .
Bombs, as well as rain, fall on the just and on the unjust."

And Andrew W. Blackwood, Jr., writes:

When a person believes in the Lord Jesus Christ, and so is saved, he
has not come to the end of his earthly struggles. There is a travesty of
Christian faith making the rounds today, to the general effect that, by
believing such and such, and doing such and such, you can become
pretty, popular, and successful. This is not Christianity, it is black

magic. . . . If you genuinely follow Jesus, who died on a cross, you will scarcely be able to avoid the normal hazards of life. . . .

Can you imagine what a hoax Christianity would be on any other basis? If belief in Christ brought good luck automatically we would have millions of pious frauds in the world, instead of the dozens we have today. Christ promises no material gain in this stage of our existence. The aim of Christian faith is Christlike character, not wealth or prominence.[2]

Fear of war is sometimes cited as a motive for giving, particularly for missions. "Send missionaries to Japan now, or send your sons as soldiers later" was a frequent cry less than a generation ago.

Now if Christian missions can deter war, and surely they can, then the Christian steward would be the last person in the world to discourage missionary giving. But suppose a Christless nation poses no military threat? What if it could be determined with certainty that a given nation would never threaten our country? Would the compassion for taking the gospel to them be lessened? Would we have any reason to give less sacrificially, to pray less devotedly?

Is there any more reason for trying to save the soul of an enemy than there is for saving the soul of a friend? Is there not equal need on the part of both?

Instead of weakening missionary giving, this approach should strengthen it. Lost men need Christ; they need him in season, out of season; they need him in war and in peace; they need him in prosperity and poverty.

Sharing the gospel costs money; we will give when the skies are darkened with war clouds and when they are filled with the doves of peace; we will give when other nations are a threat to our economic, social, or political life, and we will give when other nations are weak and powerless.

This is an ideal, yes. But the Christian steward will accept no less for a goal. While recognizing the value of controlled fear, he will seek a higher motive so that his compulsion and compassion for the ongoing of Christ's kingdom will be just as keen regardless of external world conditions and irrespective of inner, personal circumstances.

The motive of duty.—General Robert E. Lee described duty as the most sublime word in the English language. And in his *Vailima Letters*, Robert Louis Stevenson said:

The world must some day return to the word "duty," and be done with the word "reward." There are no rewards, and plenty of duties; and the sooner a man sees that and acts upon it like a Christian . . . the better for himself.

Loyalty and duty are key words in Christian discipleship. They are key words in Christian stewardship. How much of the financial support of the Lord's work rests on those faithful men and women who, week after week, are guided by an unswerving loyalty in their gifts of money. We need more loyalty, not less.

While we would recognize duty as a higher motive than fear, a word of caution is needed. Duty alone can become cold, mechanical, and legalistic. Giving can be degraded to the level of mere bill-paying. Note that element in this testimony:

"Giving to my church is my duty. No one likes to go along for a free ride. I want to pay my rightful share of the church expenses, and what it costs to give my children Christian training. Giving leaves me with a sense of pride and well-being, the feeling I have when I get all my taxes paid for the year. There is a loyalty I feel for my church, and I give it the same as I pay the grocery bills and the utilities at the end of the month."

Too, the motive of duty can lead one to be interested only in reaching a certain goal that is entirely divorced from a personal expression of stewardship. Note that element in this testimony:

"This year our church has the highest budget in its history. We have so many needs and our treasurer is always worried over unpaid bills. We simply cannot reach that budget unless more of us give liberally. Just as in my P.T.A.—when we need more funds, I get in there and help put it over. Whatever it takes—selling doughnuts, buying tickets, or serving suppers—we always reach our quota. And the church budget is even more important. We just have to reach that goal!"

Many church leaders could wish for more of their members to

share a similar loyalty, but yet they would not want them to stop at this shallow level in their motivation. Christian stewardship is far more than merely doing "my part."

The motive of self-respect.—There is some kinship with duty but the two are not synonymous.

Here is an office holder in a congregation. He observes that other church leaders consistently give more than he does. Out of self-respect, he increases his gifts. He wants his record to look better. Just as he wants to drive as nice a car as his neighbor, so he wants to give as much as his fellow teacher or deacon. There is little conception of what his money will be used for, or what relationship his giving should have to his personal worship. Again, there is simply the idea of doing "my part."

Or take the casual churchgoer with no leadership responsibilities. He goes to church "to take the kids." He had much rather hitch his boat to the back of his car come Sunday morning and head for the lake. But most of the other fathers in the block go to church (Sunday mornings) with their children, so he bows to respectability and goes too. (Of course, when they get a little older and away in school, he will go back to his Sunday fishing.)

Now the taking of the offering is one of the routines of churchgoing. It is like knotting your tie or bowing your head during the prayers. Respectable people do. So to be like everyone else, some offering is presumptuously dropped into the plate. One would be queer not to contribute.

We would not want to eliminate self-respect, but the sloven, the careless, and the don't-give-a-care members are certainly not pillars in the kingdom of God. We will stop far short in our search for Christian stewardship if we are satisfied to give only on the basis of what others will think of us.

The motive of compensation.—Occasionally a contributor is motivated by a desire to make up or compensate for his lack of service in the church. He sees others serving as ushers, singing in the choirs, teaching classes, and working on committees. He realizes he is not doing as much as others. Perhaps his explanation for not serving in some capacity is a genuine reason, or it may be a pointless excuse.

In any event, he feels that his offerings take the place of personal service.

And then occasionally, but far more rarely, one finds a person with a belligerent attitude who thinks that since the pastor is paid to do the church work, why should he be expected to help? "Let the preacher do the visiting—that's what we pay him for! What does he want to do, wait around all week to preach a couple of sermons on Sunday?"

The present-day differentiation in clergy (or paid religious workers) and laity is a rather artificial one. It is almost impossible to say, "Now that is for the pastor alone to do and this is only for the layman." The task of Christian service is one task. It is not divided into artificial compartments. We never pay anyone to do something *for* us in our churches or denomination. We do pay others to share with us the task which is the common lot of everyone. The pastor is not paid to visit for the members. He is paid to guide and assist the members in their visitation. The minister of education is not paid to teach for the members. He is paid to assist the members in their teaching task. The minister of music is not paid to sing for the congregation. He is paid to assist the congregation to sing better themselves.

There is a sense, of course, in which all giving is compensatory. Here is a consecrated businessman who would enjoy giving all his time to his church. But his family and business responsibilities demand much of his time. He gains great satisfaction as he goes about his daily work knowing that last Sunday's offering is helping to pay someone serving in a church-related vocation every day in the week. He is not paying that person to work *for* him. He has shared his money so that person can work *with* him. Every regular contributor can share the same feeling about foreign missionaries. He rejoices to know he is helping support these ambassadors of the King on foreign soil. But he also knows that world evangelization is as much his responsibility as it is the missionaries! The missionaries are not going *for* him, but rather their going is simply an enlargement and an extension of what he is trying in a limited way to do at home. It is not "your job" and "my job" but "our task!"

The motive of material gain.—This is related to the motive of fear. Just as some people give because they are afraid of punishment and retaliation if they withhold their offerings, others fear that withheld offerings will bring poverty. Hence their giving is motivated by the hope that God will reward their liberality with increased material income. This might be described also as the motive of selfishness, and include those who give to the churches because it is a "good investment" (makes the community better, discourages crime, lowers taxes and insurance, and so on).

It is certainly appealing to a base motive to promise rewards the same as one would induce obedience from children on the promise of candy. "Be good, and I'll bring you some candy! Give, and you will make more and have more!"

The hope that the more "I" give, the more "I" will get is based on a false interpretation of verses like, "Give, and it shall be given unto you" (Luke 6:38). What is forgotten is that such giving as requested in this passage includes self as well as substance. When one has given self away, then his first consideration is not gain for self but gain for others and gain for God. The person who gives on the basis of getting more in return automatically betrays a baser motive.

Real giving is not concerned with getting or with rewards, particularly the kind of rewards that can always be deposited to one's account at the local bank. There are many notable examples of liberal persons who enjoy immense material blessings, but one thing is as sure as the fact you are holding this book in your hands. *And that fact is that if such persons did their giving on the basis of anticipated returns, the rewards they gained did not come from the providence of God.* Martin Luther was not far from this subject when he commented that "Our Lord commonly giveth Riches to such gross asses, to whom he affordeth nothing else that is good."

But our purpose is not to affirm or deny that God rewards liberality. The point is that the hope of rewards should not constitute the motive for giving.

Ellis Cowling has written a very provocative booklet entitled *Let's Think About Money.* Among other good things he gives his own personal testimony on tithing, which can be used in reference to giving in general:

> To advocate tithing [or giving] on the ground that it will increase a person's income or reduce his doctor bills is dangerous. It does not always work out as promised . . . I myself grew up in a tithing family, and yet my father was plagued with ill health. There would be weeks on end when he couldn't work. We always had enough to eat and a warm home, but we experienced a number of times when we wondered how the grocer or doctor would be paid. Tithing brought neither wealth nor health to my father. He practiced it because he felt all Christians should tithe. He believed it was the Lord's will. That was enough for him. . . . When I hear men and women talking recklessly of what will happen, what near miracles have happened to them, as a result of tithing, I am moved to *remember father*, who tithed in his poverty simply because he loved the Lord.[3]

The motive of propitiation.—Occasionally someone gives to atone for his sin. If one handles a shady business deal, he then seeks to buy off God's wrath by a worthy offering! In Old Testament times, sacrifices were placed on the altar in partial or symbolical atonement for sin. But in Christian stewardship there is no room for this idea in the matter of giving.

The final spark that lit the conflagration of the Protestant Reformation was Martin Luther's condemnation of the sale of indulgences. The Roman Catholic Church was selling indulgences, or the privilege of sinning, as a means of raising funds for St. Peter's Church in Rome. One of the "peddlers," John Tetzel, would frequently say,

> Sobald der Pfenning im Iasten klingt,
> Die Seel' aus dem Fegfeuer springt.

Meaning,

> Soon as the groschen in the casket rings,
> The troubled soul from purgatory springs.

John Tetzel is long since dead, but the promise he made is still entertained in the minds of some dubious "stewards" who feel they can cover up their shortcomings by their liberality in giving.

The motive of pity.—One mother said, "At Thanksgiving and Christmas, I am always concerned that the poor have enough to eat. Somehow, our own family can enjoy the holidays better knowing others are cared for." Christian compassion? Perhaps. But perhaps an indication of concern for others only because meeting the needs of others will make possible a happy holiday!

It is one matter to have passing pity on beggars or other unfortunate persons, casting them a crumb or a coin as we hasten on our ways. It is quite another to stop, bind up their wounds, set them on our own beast, take them to an inn, and guarantee payment for their care. Which suggests the final highest motive for giving?

The motive of love.—A fireman may or may not hesitate to enter a burning building in a hopeless effort to save a child. Duty, pride, self-respect, loyalty—these virtues may force him to certain death. But there is no question about the mother of the child. She will not stop to think about duty or loyalty or pride or self-glory. She will not stop to determine whether she can return alive. Love for her child will drive her into the blinding, burning flames to place upon the altar of motherhood the gift of self. Love will find a way. Although it may be trite, there is no higher motive than love.

Love prompted the greatest Christmas Gift the world has ever received. Love drove the nails into the most precious Passover Lamb the world has ever seen. And in his immortal 1 Corinthians 13, Paul describes love as the most permanent, most beneficial of all virtues, explaining that an offering as sacrificial as one's life is absolutely nothing without the sweet-smelling odor of love.

When the risen Lord questioned Peter, he did not ask if he had graduated from a seminary. He did not ask if Peter had courage or faith. He did not question Peter's economic or social standing. There was only one question, "Do you love me?"

And that is still Christ's supreme question, both in the area of stewardship and every other phase of the Christian life. In a day when lust—whose motto is *get*—is enthroned, we need to rally around the motive of love—whose motto is *give*.

The wonderful thing about love as a motive is its undying tenacity. Love will find a way or make a way. When duty, and pride, and self-respect, and fear, and all the rest have failed, love will still find a way to express itself in the virtue of giving.

Two explorers were opening an Egyptian tomb sealed for three thousand years. It contained a beautifully carved sarcophagus of a little child. Inscribed thereon were, "Oh, my life, my love, my little one; would God I had died for thee!" The explorers silently withdrew and reverently sealed the tomb again. Parental love had lived through the years when flesh had died. They did not wish to disturb the vigil of love and death!

Love is deathless. The Christian steward seeks it as his motive for giving as he seeks it as a motive for every expression of the Christian life.

CHAPTER FIVE

HOW DO I GIVE MY MONEY?

He who would do good to another must do it in
  Minute Particulars:
General good is the plea of the Scoundrel,
  hypocrite and flatterer,
For Art and Science cannot exist but in
  minutely organized Particulars
And not in generalizing demonstrations of
  the rational power.

WILLIAM BLAKE

In the preceding chapter, attention was given to the right *sequence* in giving (self before substance) and the right *motives* for giving (love superior to fear, duty, self-respect, compensation, material gain, propitiation, or pity). Attention is now focused on the right *amount* of giving, and rightly so, for the proportionate amount one gives is directly related to his motivation. Those who give out of fear or duty, e.g., are cautious lest they "overpay," while those motivated by love experience some of the "hilarity" in giving suggested by 2 Corinthians 9:7.

A layman asked his pastor for help in determining what he should give. He had a legalistic approach, wanting to pare the amount down to the last penny. He did not want to give less than he should, but he certainly did not want to give more than his obligation. Sensing this attitude, his pastor said, "I am sorry I cannot help you. Each time you refigure, the Lord loses. When your spirit changes, I can help you."

Compare the wife who asked her husband, "Can you give me a little money?" "Yes," he replied, "how little?"

Vision of Need

When a family sets up a food budget, the first question is, "How many mouths are to be fed?" The cost for a childless couple would vary greatly from a family with ten children.

Likewise, when deciding how much to give, consider the use of the money. A great task deserves worthy financing. If the job is trivial and inconsequential, mere tipping or token giving will suffice.

Never were so few with such limited resources asked to do so much as were the believers at the ascension of Christ. They had no financial backing, no social standing, no political authority, and only a semblance of organization. They owned no church buildings, no seminaries, no publishing houses, no hospitals or other benevolent institutions. Yet Jesus commanded, "Go . . . teach all nations, baptizing them . . ." (Matt. 28:19). Earlier he had said to include healing the sick, cleansing the lepers, raising the dead, and casting out devils (Matt. 10:8).

This commission has never been revoked, for Jesus said he would be with those who obey it "even unto the end of the world." God's people are responsible for ministering to the spiritual, intellectual, and physical needs of every last man, woman, boy, and girl on the face of the earth. This ministry must be renewed with each generation. Every passing day sees the birth of new thousands needing our ministry. And if the task of the early disciples was overwhelming, no less is ours, for demographers say that one-twentieth of all the people born since Adam and Eve are alive *now!* If all these millions can be reached for Christ with sporadic, hit and miss, loose change giving, then do it! But common reasoning says this is an idle dream.

You may ask, do not these millions have their own religion? If they are sincere, isn't that enough? Jesus did not think so. He said, "I am the way, the truth, and the life: no man cometh unto the Father, but by me" (John 14:6). There is salvation and healing in only one Name. Christians know that Name and are expected to

share it. Sharing it costs money, lots of money. Those who want to
share Christ will want to give lots of money. Those who care little
or nothing about sharing him will give little or nothing. Oversim-
plified? We think not. "For where your treasure is, there will your
heart be also" (Matt. 6:21).

One must first understand that compassion for others begins
with the fellow next door. Someone says, "I envy the thrill of a missionary who goes overseas to preach to those who have never heard."
Fine! But is he willing to cross the street for Jesus? If not, it is doubtful if he would be of much service across the ocean. Another says, "I
wish I could write books and articles to convince others of the Christian way of life." Good! But will he write a post card to a Sunday
school absentee? "I wish I had a million dollars to give for missions." Wonderful! But is there willingness to give sacrificially out
of present income, week by week setting aside God's portion before
yielding to the urge to buy that new piece of furniture?

Where We Agree

In determining an amount to give, we agree initially that it
should be something. No one dares say a person could be a steward
and give nothing. But from that point opinion varies greatly.

Some say, "I want to give as I feel like it. If a cause is worthy, I'll
give what I feel it is worth." But what will happen to the lost, the
hungry, the homeless, and the ill when you don't "feel" like giving?
How do *they* feel? Imagine a mother saying, "I will feed my children when I feel like it!"

"I'll give as I'm able" says another. Basically, this is right. No one
can give what he does not own. But if one does not adopt some
standard of giving, who will say when one is "able"? Prosperity is
relative. Rare is the person who ever feels he is "able" to afford all
he wants. If one waits until all his wants are satisfied, will he ever be
"able" to give? Someone has well said that God is interested neither
in our ability nor our inability as much as he is in our availability.
This poses again the whole question of attitude.

Aside from the questions of "feeling" and "ability," there is common agreement on another factor, that giving should be propor-

tionate. "For unto whomsoever much is given, of him shall be much required" (Luke 12:48). ". . . let every one of you lay by him in store, as God hath prospered him" (1 Cor. 16:2). And the problem of proportion suggests the question of tithing.

The Origin of Tithing

The origin of the tithe—giving one-tenth of one's material increase—is lost in antiquity. Tithing is first mentioned in the Bible in Genesis 14:20, but nothing marks this as the beginning of the custom. Tithes were given to deities and political rulers by pagan nations before Abraham tithed in Genesis 14:20. The Arabians gave a tithe to the god Sabis, and the Carthaginians tithed to Melkarth, the god of Tyre. In Lydia a tithe of the cattle was given to the gods. Traces of tithing are found in Assyria and Babylonia, and early records show tithing to political rulers by the Persians, Greeks, Romans, and later the Mohammedans.

In his monumental work, *The Sacred Tenth,* Henry Lansdell says he traced tithing into almost "every known country of importance in the ancient world."

So tithing did not begin with the Mosaic law. It was almost universally practiced in the ancient pagan world as well as by early Hebrews like Abraham and Jacob. As Keil and Delitzsch point out, "All that was required was to incorporate this [tithing] in the covenant legislation, and bring it into harmony with the spirit of the law."

The Mosaic law did not limit itself to one tithe, or tenth, but included at least three distinct tithes. An elaborate system of offerings was also commanded. But one faces immediate difficulty in attempting to classify and analyze the Old Testament tithing structure. Requirements changed through the years. The task of classifying the tithe laws is more difficult since much of the time Israel existed as a theocracy, so that some of the offerings and tithes compare with modern-day taxes.

Analyzing the entire Old Testament tithing structure is almost as difficult as cataloging the income tax laws of recent years into one simple package. The changes and variations are too many. No less an authority than S. R. Driver states, "The data at our disposal do not enable us to write a history of Hebrew tithe." [1] And Joseph Marcus, writing in the *Universal Jewish Encyclopedia*, says, "The laws of the Bible in reference to the tithe are not uniform." [2] John M. Versteeg notes, "With singular unanimity biblical scholars agree as to the confusion touching the tithe." [3]

This is not said to weaken Mosaic tithing any more than it is said that tax laws are weakened because they fluctuate. There was change and adaptation, but the tithing principle was definitely established in the religious experience of Judaism. The fluctuation over the years would naturally result in difference of opinion in classifying the three tithes cited above. In broad outline, however, they followed this pattern:

The first tithe, known also as the Lord's or the Levite's or the whole tithe, consisted of one-tenth annually, whether of the seed of the land, or of the fruit of the tree, . . . the herd, or of the flock (Lev. 27:30,32). This tithe was given for support of the Levitical priesthood.

The second tithe is described in Deuteronomy 12:5–19 and 14:22–27. Three times each year the Hebrews were expected to gather at Jerusalem for the Passover, Feast of Tabernacles, and Feast of Weeks. The second tithe paid the travel and expenses of the Hebrews during their stay at Jerusalem. Tithed produce and meat were actually consumed by the worshiper as a part of the ceremony and ritual of the three feasts.

The third tithe, given only every three years and kept in the local communities for distribution to the needy (Deut. 14:28–29 and 26:12–15), was known as a charity tithe.

Counting the two annual tithes, and the third year tithe, the conscientious Hebrew gave 23⅓ per cent of his income, in addition to the prescribed offerings.

Tithing in Jesus' Day

The acceptance of the tithing structure in Jesus' day was almost universal among devout Hebrews. The proud Pharisee who recited his good deeds in the temple was careful to mention that he gave tithes (Luke 18:12). Other Pharisees were so punctilious they even tithed the leaves on the potted plants of herbs used for seasoning.

There can be no doubt that Jesus, along with Paul, Peter, and his other followers obeyed the Hebrew tithing structure as prescribed by the Judaism in which they were reared. This means they gave more than one-tenth and should not be classified as tithers in the current sense of 10 per cent givers.

Jesus' parents offered two pigeons when they presented him as a baby in the Temple. They surely trained Jesus in all of the Judaistic requirements. Jesus was criticized for breaking other laws, such as working on the Sabbath, but not for violating the law of tithes. If he had, there is no doubt he would have been criticized.

When Peter saw a vision asking him to eat food to which he was unaccustomed, he replied, "Not so Lord; for I have never eaten any thing that is common or unclean" (Acts 10:14). Strictness in this Jewish custom would suggest similar strictness in giving. Paul claimed in Philippians 3:5–6 to have been of the strictest sect of the Pharisees, which would have required obedience to the total tithing structure.

While tithing in New Testament times was an accepted custom, the New Testament is noticeably silent in its teachings regarding tithes. It mentions tithing only four times: Matthew 23:23, Luke 11:42, Luke 18:12, and Hebrews 7:4–9. (Actually only three times, as Matt. 23:23 and Luke 11:42 are parallel passages.)

Are Christians Obligated to Tithe?

There are at least three positions in answer to this question.

Legal.—Christians are just as legally bound to tithe today as the Jews were under Mosaic law.

Moral.—Christians are not legally bound to the Old Testament tithing structure, but they are morally bound to give not less than one-tenth if their Christian profession indicates any depth of consecration and sincerity.

Neither legal nor moral.—Christians are neither legally nor morally bound to tithe, and expecting one to give a tenth is far beyond the bounds of reason or of what God expects.

Very few who have made a serious study of New Testament stewardship hold to the third position. (Of course, they are greatly in the majority if we include those who practice giving less than one-tenth. But we are thinking now about serious Bible students.) More often than not, group three includes those trying to satisfy guilty consciences rather than seeking the true meaning of Christian stewardship.

Group one, who justify Christian tithing on a legalistic, obligatory basis, lean heavily on a proof-text interpretation of such passages as Malachi 3:8–10. They say that this commandment has never been repealed, and that those who withhold the tithe are God-robbers. They attach a particular sacredness to the tenth, and set it over in a special category as being separate and distinct from the other nine-tenths of one's income.

Those in group two magnify equal sacredness of the total life and of the total ten-tenths. They also point out the strong possibility that Malachi's request for tithes included the total Old Testament triple tithing structure, totaling 23⅓ per cent. They say that Malachi 3:10 does not necessarily refer to a one-tenth tithe, but that it may refer to the total Judaistic system of tithes and offerings. If so, to use the verse properly as a proof text, one would need to revert to the total tithing-offering systems of Judaism. Those who see this possibility do not feel that the principle of one-tenth tithing is weakened. Malachi does teach that God can be robbed, that man can withhold what is rightfully his. The question of interpretation is over the amount and not over the principle involved. If Malachi 3:10 refers to the total tithe-offering system of Judaism—and there is good evidence that it does—it is poor interpretation to use the verse as a proof text for one-tenth, legalistic giving.

A questionnaire was prepared, asking whether Malachi 3:10 (and also Jesus' approval of the Pharisees' tithing in Matt. 23:23) referred to one-tenth giving or to the entire Judaistic tithing structure. It was sent to a select number of professors in five Southern Baptist seminaries.

Fourteen answered the questionnaire with personal letters. Three failed to answer the question directly. Three said the passages referred to one-tenth giving (but one of them warned against using the Malachi passage as a tithing proof text). The writer understood eight of the replies to say that the passages refer to the total Judaistic tithing structure. The following statement is representative of the nine men voicing this opinion.

. . . in Malachi 3 and Matthew 23, it is absolutely arbitrary to take it that Jesus referred to one part of the tithe and not to the other two parts. There is not the slightest hint that in Matthew 23 Jesus had in mind anything less than what was clearly in the mind of the writer of Malachi 3. So that . . . if I am going to put these two Scriptures together and argue for the tithe, I should go all the way and make it the three-fold tithe, according to the teachings and practices of the Jews.

Group one, who base tithing on a legalistic requirement, frequently cite the examples of such New Testament tithers as Jesus, Paul, Peter, and the other disciples. Those in group two accept this claim as valid, but point out that the New Testament record of their tithing describes them as adherents of Judaism in the practice.

Those in group two also point out that Jesus' role was to add to the law, rather than to destroy it, and that whenever he dealt with the law he always intensified rather than minimized its requirements.

The law taught that taking another's life is murder, but Jesus said hate is murder. The law taught that sexual immorality was adultery, but Jesus said lustful desire was adultery. Now if the legalist is going to hold Jesus up as an example of a Judaistic tither, then he is saying that at this point Jesus made no improvement on the law! He would be saying that the one who warned that a righteousness superior to that of Judaism was necessary for entrance into his kingdom (Matt. 5:20) was satisfied with the righteousness of Judaism in the area of stewardship! Really, does the legalist want to say this? Does he know what he is saying when he holds up Jesus as an Old Testament tither for New Testament Christians?

Group one relies heavily on Matthew 23:23, wherein Jesus condemned the Pharisees for omitting mercy and faith, but commended them for tithing—"these ought ye to have done."

But those in group two want to know the definition of "these" and "ye." "These" is commonly interpreted as referring to giving one-tenth. But if the Pharisees were obeying the total Mosaic tithing structure, they were giving far more than one-tenth, were they not? Was not Jesus thereby commending them as *Jews* for observance of the total Jewish tithing structure? If he commended them for fulfilling the entire tithing structure, how can one take his words and say they commend one-tenth tithing? (The careful reader will also note that in Matthew 23:3, Jesus advised obedience to *all* that the scribes and Pharisees "bid you observe." If the literalist is going to use Matthew 23:23 as a proof text for tithing, then he must also explain his refusal to follow all the tenets of Judaism as recommended in Matthew 23:23.)

Look also at the meaning of "ye" in Matthew 23:23. The legalist interprets it as referring to all Christians in general. But a closer reading clearly shows he was speaking to the Pharisees. One might assume he intended all his hearers. But such is an assumption, and not what Matthew says.

This is by no means an exhaustive analysis of the different opinions about tithing. For example, no comment has been made on Hebrews 7:4–9, which some consider an important tithing passage. But enough has been said to show (1) the inadvisability of basing any doctrine on a proof-text type of interpretation and (2) that the tithing legalist stands on uncertain ground when his deductions are based on sound and accepted principles of biblical doctrine and Bible interpretation.

Should the Christian Tithe?

This is almost as obvious as, "Should a Christian tell the truth?" One would hardly conceive of a Christian wanting to give less than one-tenth when the Hebrew was often expected to give far more under Judaism. This is particularly true when the world scope of the Great Commission is compared with the often local and national Judaism!

One of the theological professors who denied the validity of legalistic tithing went on to say:

"Now, regarding tithing itself, Mrs. —— and I not only tithe, we go beyond that. . . . Since I do give to the Lord's work regularly, I need a good system to go by. . . . Just recently since . . . we have some more resources to use, we are finding great delight in going at least to twice the legal one-tenth. And we intend to do more yet. But we do not base this on a particular chapter and verse. We base it on love, our love in response to God's help."

A new convert was giving a testimony at a men's Brotherhood meeting. Commenting on his new-found joy as a tither, he said, "I wish I were able to go back and tithe all the money I earned before accepting Christ." Did he feel a compulsion, a restraint, to say that? Not at all. Rather it was the joyful cry of a man who had found so much joy in planned, proportionate giving that he regretted what he had been missing through the years.

Some might feel this approach weakens stewardship. Rather, it strengthens it. Is there more power in force than love? Is law greater than grace? Is legalism more compulsive than personal salvation? Another professor writes:

I am deeply concerned about the tendency among Southern Baptists to refuse the responsibility of freedom in Christ under grace. We seem to be afraid of freedom and therefore we are inclined to put ourselves under law. To teach our people that tithing is the Christian way of stewardship is to deny our people the right to be full-grown, mature people in the kingdom of God. So long as we treat them as children they will act as children and remain immature Christians. We must challenge them to accept the responsibilities of grace and freedom and teach them full, all-encompassing stewardship in the kingdom of God.

When giving is placed on this basis, then the sincerity of one's Christian profession is at stake in the proportionate amount he gives. The question eventually resolves itself to: Could one possibly give less than a tenth and expect others to take seriously his Christian profession? C. H. Spurgeon was asked, "Are the heathen saved without the gospel?" He answered, "The main question is not whether they can be saved without the gospel, but whether I can claim salvation and withhold the gospel from them."

This places tithing not on willingness to obey a stipulated law but on the genuineness of one's Christian experience. If the giving of one-tenth as a minimum can be placed on surer footing than one's Christian profession, we are waiting for it to be suggested!

Law or no law, legalism or no legalism—even take a pair of scissors and cut from the Bible every verse dealing with tithing—one is still challenged to say he is a sincere disciple and refuse to give at least one-tenth of his income to the cause which he says, by his professed discipleship, is the most important in the world.

It is time to recognize that the nontither is failing to give at least one-tenth not because he is afraid of legalism, but because he wants the money more for something else. He wants a newer model car, a longer vacation, dressier clothes, newer furniture, more elaborate sporting goods. Valuable time can be saved when this fact is recognized rather than arguing over whether Jesus taught tithing. (Someone has said the average preacher spends too much time anyway answering questions that no one ever asks.)

Many stewards hold to a rigid minimum of one-tenth because they recognize the frailties of human emotion. "Sometimes I'm up, sometimes I'm down." One gets greatly excited about all he is going to give, but yet refuses to adopt a proportionate minimum. Then he hits a "down" period. He temporarily loses his vision. His giving will suffer unless he follows a set formula for a minimum.

Unless one begins somewhere he will end up nowhere. A Japanese proverb reads, "A journey of a thousand miles begins with one step." He knows, as F. B. Meyer explained, that he will never give all he wants to give in his higher moments of inspiration unless he is "minute, and specific, and careful." "He who would do good . . . must do it in Minute Particulars."

Does Tithing Pay?

The answer depends on what one means by "pay." One writer says, "Tithing, if conscientiously practiced, absolutely guarantees material blessings." He also says, "These promises (Mal. 3:10) constitute nothing less than a holy insurance policy with heavenly security. The insurance is against disaster, misfortunes, poverty, drouth, boll weevil, and any other adversity to man." [4] And another writes:

> One *tenth* for the Lord and *nine* for you
> It isn't so very much to do
>> And perchance the tenth may soon come back
>> In heavenly favor; so—where's your lack?
> Join the Tither's League
>> If God gets His and I get mine
>> Then everything will be just fine.
>
> ANONYMOUS

The question of rewards is not quite that simple, for it poses a more difficult question, that of suffering. As Frank K. Means has so well said, "The solid fact, however distasteful it may be, is that the righteous are not always and uniformly prosperous. Their prosperity is rooted in the spiritual rather than the material. The same canon which contains the third chapter of Malachi also contains the story of Job, the twelfth chapter of Jeremiah, and the seventy-third Psalm." [5]

Notwithstanding the numerous and sincere testimonies of tithers who got salary increases as soon as they started tithing, the Bible still teaches that a good man can and often does suffer. Jesus made this clear in his discussion with the Jews about the possibility of a rich man being saved. When he said it was easier for a camel to go through the eye of a needle than for a rich man to enter heaven, they were amazed. They thought wealth was always a sign of God's favor, and poverty a sign of God's disfavor. If a rich man (evidently basking in God's favor) had difficulty getting into heaven, who *could* be saved? Jesus was not saying the rich could not be saved, but he was saying that wealth was not always a sign of favor for meritorious living. Why say, then, that it "pays to tithe?"

Yes, it does "pay" to tithe, if by payment one means a satisfied conscience, a joy in knowing one's dollars are at work day and night winning men to Christ; or if one means a keener appreciation for and better management of money or God's privilege to bestow material blessings, if and when he chooses.

No, a thousand times no, it does not pay to tithe if one means "insurance" against all known catastrophes, an increase in income for every step-up in giving, fewer doctor bills and immunity from accidents. This "No" is sounded from the ash heap where sits Job scraping his boils with a potsherd, a man whose only fault that Satan could find was his faith in God. This "No" echoes from Calvary where writhes in agony One who gave not a tenth but all that he had, and whose only reward was the spittle of his jeerers and the piercing nails of his executioners.

This is not said to deny the validity of unnumbered testimonies of conscientious tithers whose cups have been filled to overflowing in their practice of Christian stewardship. It is said to warn against the promise of material rewards as a motive for giving, and to resay that sometimes adversity is a reward and bitterness a blessing.

Samuel E. Maddox, son of missionary parents, tells an experience that beautifully expresses the Christian position on rewards.

His parents, Mr. and Mrs. O. P. Maddox, had just returned to Rio de Janerio in 1914 from furlough. The customs officials, thinking they were wealthy American business people, pronounced such high import duties that the missionaries were unable to claim their luggage. Little did these officials dream that the annual salary of this couple was a mere four hundred dollars, plus travel and housing.

Some time later Mrs. Maddox was bathing their one-year-old son. She left him a few moments to answer the door. When she returned, the child had drowned. In an effort to revive the lifeless form, four doctors worked unsuccessfully for two hours.

Following the burial, as they were getting into the carriage for the return trip into the city, Mrs. Maddox said, "What is this strange joy that I feel in my heart on this darkest day of our lives?" Mr. Maddox replied, "This is Christ's promise to be with us to the end of the age!"

The next day's mail brought exorbitant bills from the four doctors (who also thought they were wealthy) and their small salary check. For the first time in his life, Mr. Maddox wondered whether it would be right to withhold some of their tithe. Mrs.

Maddox spoke up, "No, let us give as we always have. Even if we used our tithe, it would not begin to meet our obligations."

To make a long story short, friends intervened, the doctor bills were greatly reduced, and the customs removed. But the greatest victory was not in God's providence in helping meet their bills—it was the faith he gave this missionary couple to say, "God is first in our lives."

Their son, Dr. Samuel Maddox, in commenting on this experience says, "When father and mother died, they had very little of this world's goods, but they left me with a priceless heritage, a memory of parents who dared to put God first in all of life's experiences."

Determining the Tithe

Once an individual decides to tithe, he faces the question of how to determine one-tenth of his income. Are there certain logical deductions? If so, what? What about taxes, medical expenses, etc.? The last thing anyone wants to do is write a rule book on tithing. Jesus directed one of his most stinging rebukes at the Pharisees with their detailed plans for figuring the tithe. However, basic principles can be given. Beyond this, each person must work out his specific problems.

Principle one.—Do not say you are a tither unless you give one-tenth of your *total income.* This should go without saying, but it is doubtless true that some church members consistently claim to give one-tenth, knowing that their actual gifts, Sunday after Sunday, are far below the tithe.

Principle two.—The tithe is not a tax. Unfortunately, some have compared the tithe to income tax, with elaborate suggestions for figuring deductions, allowances, refunds, etc. One who determines his tithe on the basis of "How little I can give" is likely to violate the whole spirit of tithing.

Principle three.—A tither will give one-tenth of all his increase; i.e., of anything that comes into his possession which benefits him in a material way. This increase may come in many forms: as income, gifts, interest, rents, royalties, honorariums, payments, capital gains, bequests, inheritances, bonuses, judgments, awards, etc. Unfortunately, many a person on wages or salaries never stops to consider the amount of his total income. He may think that salary consists only of the amount of money actually received in the pay check. He often overlooks the fact that the employer is acting only as his agent in withholding enough to pay income tax, Social Security, insurance, etc. But this money is withheld from the *employee's* earnings to pay the *employee's* obligations.

Someone answers, "But I never have the money in my possession, therefore I do not figure it is my responsibility to tithe it." All right, why not ask your employer to withhold enough to pay your food bill, car payments, etc.? Thus, you could "save" even more on your tithe! Such reasoning, of course, is ridiculous, and is simply mentioned to show the absurdity of saying that money withheld is not a part of one's actual income. A conscientious tither will secure from his employer—if he does not know already—the amount of his total earnings before deductions, when making his pledge to tithe.

Principle four.—A tither may logically deduct legitimate expenses in securing his income. (The word "deduct" has some objectionable feature, but is used here for lack of a clearer term.) The only problem is in defining "legitimate expenses." In the end, each Christian must decide this in the light of his conscience and the leadership of the Holy Spirit. This may help: A legitimate expense is one that is over and above the normal expenses of daily life that one would expect to incur whether he were digging ditches or building a skyscraper! One would expect, e.g., to spend a nominal amount for transportation to work as a regular expense of "living." But extensive travel in connection with one's work would not be a regular expense of normal living, and hence would not be tithed. One would expect, for example, to pay taxes and insurance premiums on his home and family as a part of normal living, regardless of his vocation. But taxes and insurance on business property would be a peculiar expense of doing business and would not be tithed. A mother who must work to support her children or an invalid husband might not give a tithe on the amount required for a housekeeper or maid. But a wife who chose to work simply to get away from the routine of homemaking would want to give a tithe of the money she spent on extra help. Other examples might be cited, but these should suffice to illustrate the principle.

Principle five.—Those who have the most difficulty in determining the tithe are often those who do not wish to tithe anyway, and are only looking for ways to "save" on the tithe and still maintain a clear conscience.

Keeping One's Pledge

Living expenses are high and inflation continues to eat its way into one's purse. Where is one going to find the money to meet his pledge to tithe? Four suggestions are given:

Faith.—One's pledge to tithe is a venture in faith. The future is uncertain for all of us: sickness, loss of employment, change of income, retirement, and so on, which means that all of life is a venture. It is filled with uncertainty and change. But the conscientious tither thinks of his life as a partnership with God. He asks God to give him health and strength to work. He knows that he does not face the responsibilities of life alone.

Not presumption.—This means that the tither does not presume that God will always provide the money for the tithe, regardless of whether the tither works or tries to budget his money. Tithing is not an unemployment insurance policy. Tithers do not always get a raise in salary to offset their pledges! To depend on such would be presumption, not faith.

Family budgeting.—Most families will find it easier to tithe if they will work out a budget for all their home expenses. The tithe should be included as a major item, along with food, clothing, insurance, utilities, etc. The amount for the tithe should be set aside for that purpose, and not used for anything else. In developing a budget, distinguish between your family's *needs* and their *wants*. Most of us never catch up with our wants. The more we earn, the more we want. If you wait until you can buy all you *want* before tithing, you will likely never tithe!

Determination.—You can follow the above suggestion by deter-

mining to *live on what you earn.* You might like to live better and
have more. But until you earn more, accept a standard of living in
line with your earnings. You will be much happier, and your family
will be more content. You will thus refuse to worship at the shrine
of the "adoration of the unpossessed." If this means one must
lower his standard of living (shorter vacations, fewer steaks, older
cars) in order to tithe, such would not be inconsistent with the example of One who gave not one-tenth, but all He had for us and
our salvation. Determine your tithe in the shadow of Calvary, and
you will not go far amiss. And remember—if you are unwilling to
tithe your present income, it is doubtful if you would tithe a higher
one!

Sharing the Tithe

Another very practical question that often arises is how to divide
the tithe among the children. The Bible gives no rules on this
question. Each family must decide what is best. Here are three ways
that families commonly share the tithe:

Plan A.—One tenth of the total family income is divided equally
among the parents and children. If there are five in the family, and
the weekly tithe totals $15, each person makes a weekly gift of $3.

Plan B.—Some parents feel it is too great a responsibility to ask
a Beginner child, e.g., to take $3 to church. They divide the major
part of the tithe between the parents, and a lesser share with the
children, depending on their age. With a tithe of $15, each parent
might give $7, and the remaining $1 shared with the children.

Plan C.—Other parents divide the tithe equally among themselves, and teach the children to give one-tenth of their allowances
or earnings. Thus, with a tithe of $15, each parent would give $7.50.
If one child had an allowance of $1 weekly, he would give ten
cents, etc.

Which plan is best? There are good reasons for each one. Each
family must make its own decision. Of more importance is the
decision to start tithing—now! Determine to give the tithe top
priority in your spending habits, and most of the problems of procedure, etc., will take care of themselves.

There's a way to face the future,
    There's a way to leave the past.
There's a way to form a habit,
    There's a way to make it last.

There's a million ways of starting
    And a million ways to stop;
But the way to do your tithing
    Is to take it off the top! [6]
                        PETER E. LONG

This completes step four in the stewardship of material possessions, "How do I give my money?" Granted this step is successfully taken, one is ready for step five, "How do I spend my money?"

CHAPTER SIX

HOW DO I SPEND
MY MONEY?

> A vain man's motto is: Win gold and wear it.
> A generous man's: Win gold and share it.
> A miser's: Win gold and hoard it.
> A prodigal's: Win gold and spend it.
> A broker's: Win gold and lend it.
> A gambler's: Win gold and lose it.
> A Christian's: Win gold and use it.

> The use of money is all the advantage
> there is in having money. Wealth is not
> his who has it, but his who enjoys it.
>
> BENJAMIN FRANKLIN

A young housewife was disturbed because small children and home responsibilities limited her church work. One day she offered a personal check to the postman for a C.O.D. package. He replied, "Although it is against postal regulations, I will take your personal check. I believe I can trust you, for I have noticed from your mail how prompt you are in paying bills. Some of your neighbors get repeated notices before meeting their obligations. You only get a bill one time!" She was somewhat surprised as well as pleased. Unconsciously, she had been witnessing for Christ in the *spending* of her money.

This suggests step five in the stewardship of material possessions, "How do I spend my money?"

Some might protest, "If I give at least one-tenth, then it is my business how I spend what is left." On the contrary, one's spending habits reveal his stewardship as keenly as one's giving habits. More dollars and cents are involved, and the lives of more people are touched. Improper spending habits could mar one's record of liberality, or they could give added emphasis to this virtue.

Going a Step Further

Looking at the spending of money in contrast with the giving of money on a purely mathematical basis, the former is much more important than the latter. Assume that one is a tither, and conscientiously gives one-tenth of his total income through his church. This leaves nine-tenths for personal use—on himself, his family, savings, etc. In other words, the tither has nine times as many opportunities to be a Christian steward in the use of his money as he has in the giving of it!

If one accepts the principle of total accountability, then he cannot but admit this truth. On the other hand, if one is going to limit stewardship to tithing, he will regard the giving of the one-tenth as the chief expression of stewardship.

Which is more nearly correct? The thesis of this book from the beginning has been that stewardship includes the total resources of life, both personal and material. Granted the truth of this, the use of the nine-tenths, mathematically speaking, is of greater importance than giving the one-tenth. This is not said to imply that the tithe is so insignificant that one needn't bother in giving it. But it is said to magnify the fact that one cannot give a tenth on Sunday and then proudly tell himself that he has disposed of his financial obligations to God. God, who owns the cattle on a thousand hills, is not a beggar, dependent on our tithes. But he is our heavenly Father, who wants us to follow the principle of accountability in the use of every penny that comes into our possessions.

The average family in the United States is said to have a lifetime income of $250,000. (The income of some is much higher. For example, an annual income of $7,500 from age twenty through sixty-five would amount to more than $330,000 in a lifetime. For others, the total is much smaller. An annual income of $3,000 from age twenty through sixty-five would be $215,000.)

Taking the $250,000 lifetime income as an average, it is estimated that $58,000 is spent on housing and $48,000 for food and drink. Taxes claim $36,000, and $26,000 goes for church, clubs, and education. The family car requires $24,000, insurance $16,000, clothing $12,000, and recreation $12,000. Medical bills total $6,000 with $12,000 going for miscellaneous items.

Thus, the average family is seen as giving far less than even one-tenth to the church. But granted a full $25,000 was given through one's church, look at the thousands of dollars spent on housing, food, recreation, clothing, transportation, and insurance. Think of the hundreds and even thousands of business transactions within the average lifetime. Consider the shelves of books and magazines, the barrels of gasoline, the quantities of food, the closets of clothing one purchases. Each purchase of goods, each payment for services rendered, and each bill remitted becomes an opportunity to practice Christian stewardship.

Is it good stewardship to buy pulp magazines when one could invest in top-quality books? Is it good stewardship to burn gasoline for aimless driving when one could take his family to see worthwhile places? Is it good stewardship to spend one's money for body-harming drugs and beverages, when he could buy healthful goods with the same money? Or to give way to impulse buying of gourmet foods while thousands suffer from malnutrition?

> Our garbage man comes twice a week—
> (City law forbids the reek)
> In summer, every day.
>
> But, Oh, I ask; does He forgive
> That somewhere little ones could live
> On what we throw away? [1]
>   MILDRED R. BENSMILLER

The spending of money surely becomes, then, a major facet of Christian stewardship.

Money Is a Tool

The spending of money includes the management of money. And the wise management of money, whether it is saved, spent, given, or invested, is just about as important as the amount of money one earns. Quite frequently a person with a lower income has a higher standard of living then one with a better income. The difference is in management. A careful steward learns well how to manage money so that it will achieve the most possible good for himself and others.

Back in 1270 Thomas Aquinas said that "The art of acquiring money is subordinate to the art of using money," which suggests that in stewardship common sense is needed more than copper cents! And C. H. Spurgeon said, "A fool may make money, but it needs a wise man to spend it." Henry Ford pointed out that the use of money is so vital that it could be compared with an arm or a leg —use it or lose it. Which brings to mind the oft-quoted claim that we either *use, lose,* or *misuse* our God-given blessings.

Money is consecrated or desecrated by its use. It assumes many roles and wears many guises, depending on the user that handles it.

> Dug from the mountain-side, washed in the glen,
> Servant am I or the master of men.
> Steal me, I curse you,
> Earn me, I bless you;
> Grasp me and hoard me, a fiend shall possess you.
> Lie for me, die for me, covet me, take me—
> Angel or devil, I am what you make me.[2]
>
> ARTHUR GUITERMAN

In spending money, the Christian steward is not to think that money is evil and that personal enjoyment of what it can purchase is a sin. It is the misuse, not the use, of money which is sinful. Jesus taught, "I am come that they might have life, and that they might have it more abundantly" (John 10:10). Not nearly all of the elements of the abundant life can be purchased with money, but neither are we to divorce from the abundant life any identification whatsoever with the material. Guy L. Morrill means this when he writes:

> The new Christian asceticism will not be based on the false premise that the material world is evil *per se* nor on the pagan idea that pain, privation, and lack have in themselves spiritual worth which does not and cannot inhere in plenty, in comfort, and in joy. . . . God does not ask for a renunciation, a relinquishment, an abandonment, a giving up of his gifts. He asks for their dedication, their consumption, their management, their use in terms of a partnership with him. . . . We are going to find the way to make our abundance achieve life's best for us and for all men.[3]

The Virtue of Frugality

To say that money is a servant to be enjoyed does not give license for overspending, selfish indulgence, and a devil-may-care attitude. Careful spending and saving habits are marks of Christian character as surely as liberality. This is true because the one who dissipates his money will soon find he is dissipating himself.

Jesus commended prudence and thrift in the parables of the ten virgins and the unjust steward. The five virgins, with no foresight beyond immediate needs, found themselves shut out from the wedding feast. The unjust steward who anticipated tomorrow's needs found the answer in wise use of the money he possessed.

"Make a little money first, then make a little money last" is always good advice. The idea of thrift was suggested in a motto carved on the kitchen fireplace of Sir Walter Scott's home at Abbotsford. It read simply, "Waste not, want not." And many modern homes could profit from the old proverb, "Eat it up! Make it do! Do without!" The advice may sound old-fashioned, but following it would put many a home on sounder economic footing. Too many times we find ourselves spending money we do not have to buy things we do not need to keep up with people we do not like. In the face of abundance, following the feeding of the five thousand, Jesus was careful to see that twelve baskets of leftovers were carefully gathered.

The great Creator, who did not waste a single leaf or blade of grass as he pressed the vegetation of countless centuries into the bowels of the earth to make coal and other natural resources for today's industry, is our supreme example. To waste is to destroy, and destruction of anything has always been contrary to the Christian concept of the sacredness of human life and every other product of God's creative hand.

The temptation to live beyond one's means is a constant one, encouraged by the pressure of modern advertising. This is not said to condemn advertising, which is a service that continually improves our standard of living by introducing new products and creating in the consumer a desire for better products. The harm lies with the consumer who yields to the pressure and makes purchases beyond his ability. Easy credit and the numerous time-payment plans join hands with advertising to lead the unsuspecting buyer to commit himself beyond his ability.

The homespun philosopher was right when he said, "Next t'pickin' up a safety-razor blade with a boxin' glove on, th' hardest thing to meet is them 'easy' payments."

Don't Go Too Far!

Whereas Jesus condemned the squandering of wealth in the story of the prodigal son, his parable of the rich fool counseled against hoarding. One can be unchristian in the matter of frugality if he stoops to miserliness. Let no one say that because he is overly-cautious in his saving habits he is thereby a Christian steward. Christian thrift is not merely saving money for a rainy day. Frugality includes prudent spending as well as prudent saving. Because one has learned how to "save money" does not automatically classify him as a Christian steward.

> . . . thrift itself
> May be a sort of slow, unwholesome fire
> that eats away to dust the life that feeds it.[4]

So agrees Guy L. Morrill, "Thrift then is not merely having a bank account; it is taking care of what one has. It is the planned use of all one's resources to insure the utmost return in their expenditure." [5] And someone else has said that it is always false economy to deny one's self necessary things today in order to buy unnecessary things tomorrow!

Recall the young man who became so enthusiastic over finding a five dollar bill on the street. It gave him so much "pleasure" that from that time on he never looked up while walking. During his lifetime he accumulated 29,519 buttons, twenty-two cents, 54,172 pins, a bent back, and a miserly disposition. It is safe to say that many of his relatives are still living! They have become so enamored with the accumulation of wealth that they have forgotten the Christian use of wealth.

There was a man in our town
    And he had wondrous health;
But recklessly he squandered it
    Accumulating wealth.
And when he saw his health was gone,
    With all his might and main,
He squandered all the wealth he'd won
    To get his health again.
And when with neither health nor wealth,
    He in his coffin lay;
The preacher couldn't say a thing
    Excepting, "Let us pray!" [6]

Miserliness—stinginess—greed—covetousness! These are bedfellows which the conscientious steward will avoid. He knows that it is possible even to be a tither and still void his testimony by succumbing to the wiles of this quartet of vices.

The good steward will avoid miserliness, knowing that it is a form of idolatry. He knows that the miser is simply an idol whose greatest joy is in counting his money, feeling it run through his fingers, and feasting his eyes on it. He will avoid stinginess, the trait that dries up the springs of generosity and encourages one to hold on to everything he gets.

Likewise he will avoid greed, the third partner in the quartet, because he refuses to stoop so low as to be compared with the pig at a trough which is never satisfied with his share, regardless of the amount.

Finally, he steers clear of covetousness, that sin which tempts one to steal, lie, kill, or deceive in order to take what rightfully belongs to another.

One of the sad things about the miserly type of individual who thinks that money is made only to be saved is the unhappiness in his own life. Thomas Fuller said that "Great wealth and content seldom live together." Seneca noted that "It is not the man who has too little, but the man who craves more, that is poor." What the miser fails to recognize is that the world has enough for everyone's need but not enough for everyone's greed.

A very conservative old couple owned a lovely furnished house. One day the wife called, "Joseph, where are you?" "I'm resting in the parlor." "What, on the sofy?" she cried, horrified. "No, on the floor." Then in anguish, "Not on that grand carpet?" "No, I've rolled it up!"

One woman lived in constant fear someone would break in and steal her beautiful silver. For twenty years she had been nudging her husband at night, saying, "Get up, John, I believe someone is downstairs and they may get my silver." On one of those rare nights when he obeyed, John actually found a burglar. He introduced himself to the intruder and then suggested, "My brother, I want you to come upstairs and meet my wife. She has been looking for you for twenty years!"

And then there was the cautious, conservative, frugal individual who passed away. Someone asked a neighbor the cause of his death. "I don't know," he answered, "unless he died of too much self-restraint!"

But blinding, grinding miserliness is not a joke. The tenth commandment forbids covetousness, and Paul took it seriously enough to classify it with adultery. "For this ye know, that no whoremonger, nor unclean person, nor covetous man, who is an idolater, hath any inheritance in the kingdom of Christ" (Eph. 5:5, Goodspeed). Why describe a man as successful then simply because he has learned to build a sizable bank account? He may be blind and

insensible to all the finer values of life about him. As William
Blake noted:

To the eye of a miser a guinea is far more beautiful than the sun and
a bag worn with the use of money has more beautiful proportions than
a vine filled with grapes. As a man is, so he sees.

Then he added his own testimony:

When the sun rises, do you not see a round disk of fire something
like a gold piece? O no, no, I see an innumerable company of the
Heavenly host crying Holy, Holy, Holy is the Lord God Almighty.

Worthy Ways

It would be presumptuous to suggest to each reader how to
spend his money in harmony with the principles of Christian stewardship. Motive and intent and attitude are more important than
rules. Each individual must work out his own formula and pattern
and budget spending.

Much has already been said about saving, and saving money is
rightly a phase of spending. Some follow the old adage, "Give a
tenth and save a tenth." Those who practice it say it is not a bad
idea. One must be careful to define "savings." Cash on deposit in
a savings account at the bank is but one of many methods for saving. Investments, real estate, insurance, retirement programs, personal property—all of these may rightly be classed as savings.

Certainly one should spend enough and spend wisely to care for
the physical needs of himself and his dependents. It is false economy to deny one's self or one's family proper food only to spend it
later for medicine. Money wisely spent on housing, recreation,
medical care, travel, education, clothing, and food is a wise investment. One's income, vocation, and the accepted standard of living in his community are factors to be considered.

One danger to guard against is of waiting until "tomorrow" to
provide the things one desires for his family. This may be due to a
driving fear of dependency on charity or relatives in old age. If so,

one may rob his family of today's necessities to make possible tomorrow's security.

In all due respect to the need for providing for old age, the chief aim in life is not to retire to a rocking chair with a comfortable nest egg nearby! Yet many are determined to vacation in Europe after retirement, even if they have to go in a wheelchair. Financial independence may be desirable, but it is a poor goal for an immortal soul made in the image of God!

Besides, can one live on money alone when he comes to retirement? What about memory? He may be unable to travel and enjoy his money in old age as he planned. All he may do is reminisce. What treasured memories will he have—memories of weekly trips to the local bank? Not very good fare for an oldster, is it? Compare the individual who provides for tomorrow, but also enjoys today. He spends some of his money for personal and family enjoyment while he can benefit from it. Investments are made in education, in medical care, in good food, in travel and recreation. The declining years are happier years because they are filled with memories of a good life.

Life must be lived as we go along, or it will never be lived. And it costs some money to live! Here is a man who skimps on medical or educational care for his child or companion. He can invest a dollar today and ten years from now have two dollars. Then he will buy what his family needs. But in ten years he may have the two dollars but not the loved one. If so, it would matter little if his dollar had increased to a thousand.

> But O for the touch of a vanish'd hand,
> And the sound of a voice that is still.[7]

Wise parents recognize that "life is short if the early years are lost." The ten cent balloon they refuse their child today will never have the same appeal again, even though they are able to buy them by the hundreds after their children are grown.

One office worker carefully invested her money for retirement years. Some days she would miss lunch to meet her insurance. She died just as she was ready to retire. A distant relative who had cared little for her during her lifetime claimed what she had worked so hard to save.

This is not to discredit insurance, savings, or retirement programs. It is only to say that everyone does not live to retire, and many of those who retire do not know how to live! Life must be lived as we go along.

Poverty's Children

"But neither spending nor saving is a problem—every penny is already committed before I receive it," someone answers.

Then remember, there can be some satisfaction in the money one does not have. Poverty's children know some joys their richer cousins never experience. So noted Stephen B. Elkins, "Rich men never whistle, poor men always do."

And simply because one earns much is no reason he can consume so much more than anyone else. An old proverb reads, "Though your threshing-floor grind out a hundred thousand bushels of grain, not on that account will your stomach hold more than mine."

An old Negro woman who was always gay and cheerful was asked her philosophy of life. Her explanation (which noticeably excluded dependence on money), "Lawd, chile, I jes' weahs de worl' lak a loose gyarment!"

Dr. J. R. Grant, onetime president of Ouachita Baptist College in Arkansas, describes a father and mother who brought their pampered boy to his office. In the boy's presence they said, "Here is our son. He has failed in two colleges, but we have determined to give him an education so he won't have to work as we have." Dr. Grant did what he could, but the boy failed a third time.

"So he won't have to work!" As if work, and sacrifice, and doing without were a disgrace.

It is good to thank God occasionally for what we do not have, as well as what we do have. The absence of life's things often makes it possible to see life's realities. C. Powell, Jr., of Philadelphia, Pennsylvania, shares this helpful experience:

I do outside construction work and sometimes, when things are slow and with six kids to feed, money is plenty scarce. Last week's pay was smaller than usual, three of the kids had worn out their shoes and, to top it off, the washing machine finally gave up the struggle and died. It was one of those times when you wonder why you keep plugging away, year after year.

I bought the new shoes and went to look at a secondhand washing machine. The family selling it seemed to have everything—new automatic washer, drier and dishwasher. After I arranged to pick up their old washer in the kids' wagon the next day, our conversation turned to children and I began grumbling about the high price of shoes and how quickly the kids wore them out. The woman looked at her husband and walked away. When she was out of earshot he told me that their only child was paralyzed and had never walked a step.

When I got home I picked up the worn-out shoes—Joe's with the tips completely gone from using them as brakes on his wagon, Clair's from skipping rope, and little Jim's still wet from jumping into every puddle of water he could find. That night I gave thanks to my Maker for the worn-out shoes in our house.[8]

Money and Family Happiness

"Silver Threads Among the Gold" was written around the turn of the century by Hart P. Danks in tribute to a happy home and family. The song was an unexpected hit, and the royalties poured in. But there was disagreement over how to spend the new-found wealth. Separation followed. Danks died alone in a rooming house in Philadelphia. Nearby was found an old copy of the song with these words written across it, "It's hard to grow old alone."

Dissention over how to spend the family income has wrecked more than one home. Regardless of the amount involved, it can be a joyous, co-operative venture or it can be a nightmare of suspicion, disagreement, and wrangling. "Better is a dinner of herbs where love is, than a stalled ox and hatred therewith" (Prov. 15:17). Or in modern speech, "Better a supper of cold beans where love is, than prime ribs of beef and hatred therewith." Or in the words of John Ray "A little house well-fill'd, a little land well-till'd, and a little wife well-will'd, are great riches."

One source of family friction over finances is what Ellis Cowling describes as the adoration of the unpossessed:

The house we now live in, the car already in our garage, the current furnishings in our homes, serve their purpose, and we are sure we couldn't get along with anything older or less expensive. But we are equally convinced that if we had something finer, newer, larger, more expensive, different from what we have now, we would be much better pleased with it and with ourselves. We adore what we don't own.[9]

He goes on to say that most people feel that if they could earn just a little bit more, they would be satisfied. If they earned what their neighbor did, their worries would be ended. What they fail to see is that their neighbor probably feels the same way! The constant urge for more and the unrelenting desire for the unpossessed are two unsolved problems in many homes today.

The late William Temple, one time Archbishop of Canterbury, recognized the evil of materialism as a problem for all society as well as the home when he said:

This world today is much like a hardware store in which by night a joker breaks in and mixes up the price tags. When the owner enters the store the next morning he finds lawn mowers are marked two for five cents; nails twenty-five cents each and a gallon of paint for one penny. That is what has happened to our civilization today. We shall not come to order and peace in our world until our price tags tally with God's.

The Family Budget

A sound family budget can often help one to be a good steward in the spending of money. Unfortunately, some people shy away from budgets because they think that a budget is primarily a device for *saving* money and that it will therefore rob them of the enjoyment of buying the things they want.

Actually, the opposite is true. The chief purpose of a family budget is *discipline*, not economy. A budget enables a family to adjust its spending habits so money will be available for the things they want most. Saving money might be one of the aims—or even the chief aim—of a family budget. But not necessarily so. One might conceivably operate his home very efficiently on a budget and save little.

If a family desires an extended vacation, a budget will help accumulate the money needed. If the family wants an educational fund for the children, or savings for retirement, or new furniture for the dining room—then a budget can discipline them to reserve funds for these objects rather than aimless, spasmodic spending.

For the Christian steward, the family budget becomes a tool to guide in the wise spending of money so that the basic needs of each member of the family is met; and to enable them to set aside one-tenth or more for church offerings. The fact that a person spends according to a budget is no guarantee he is a good steward, because he might budget his expenditures to omit completely his church and/or to provide for desirable, but non-essential wants at the expense of basic needs.

Here are some basic steps in family budgeting:

First, know the exact amount of one's disposable income, i.e., take home pay.

Second, decide to make the budget total less than one's income to allow for emergencies and overlooked items. (Junior will break an arm, the car battery will go dead, or the plumbing will spring a leak!)

Third, distinguish between family *needs* and family *wants*. List first the obligations that must be met (the tithe, housing, clothing, food, transportation, medical, taxes, insurance). Provide for these first.

Fourth, list the family *wants*. These are optionals which will be purchased if there is money after the *needs* are met (a newer model car, more fashionable clothing, longer vacations, etc.). Most families have budget trouble because of inability to distinguish between *needs* and *wants*. Advertising, social pressure, etc., often influence one to spend "need" money for "wants."

Fifth, adopt a sane flexibility. Straining to make the budget come out even to the last penny is so frustrating that it often causes a family to ditch the budget in disgust and go back to haphazard spending. Burning a half gallon of gasoline and wasting fifteen minutes to drive across town to save two cents on ten pounds of sugar is not sound budgeting any more than sound dieting consists of drinking tea without sugar (saving about 40 calories) and then eating two slices of cherry pie (750 calories) for dessert!

The use of charge accounts makes it possible for some families to operate more or less on a budget. A family sets a "credit ceiling" at a department store. Payments are so much per month. Thus, the family buys up to the ceiling, and budgets the monthly payments.

But this is not necessarily the best kind of family budgeting, unless one is willing to pay for the discipline enforced by such charge accounts. For more often than not, there are carrying charges to such accounts. But a housewife replies, "My charge account enables me to take advantage of sales when I might not have the cash." This is true, if. . . . Suppose, for example, a $25 coat is on sale for $17. The purchaser "saves" $8. But more often than not, the same shopper will use the $8 to buy another item, i.e., will repeatedly spend each month up to her credit ceiling. Perhaps the $8 item was needed, and perhaps not. But if one gives in purely to impulse buying in spending the other $8, he has actually saved nothing. But he will pay carrying charges on the entire $25.

The same is true when one buys an item purely because of the saving offered. Notice the number of newspaper ads that cry, "Save $3, or $20, or $100." The emphasis seems to be not so much on the quality of the advertised item, as the appeal to the buyer's innate desire to save. If one purchases, e.g., a $3.98 item he does not need for $1.98, he has supposedly saved $2.00. Actually, he has wasted the $1.98 he paid, for that money could have been used to purchase something he really wanted, *even though it was not on sale*. Does one shop to save money, or, to meet his needs and wants?

The same principle holds true among the growing numbers of persons who rely on small loan companies. Often a family will secure a loan, make a few payments, and then refinance. The balance of the loan is never paid off, but the monthly payments become a kind of family budget. Again, if one is willing to pay high interest rates for the "discipline" of regular payments, such loans are probably good. But think how much more one could have for his money if he saved in advance and paid cash, thus getting full benefit for both the amount previously paid for interest as well as principal.

The high cost of small loans is often overlooked. A current newspaper advertisement gives this schedule:

You Get	18 Payments	24 Payments
$ 100	$ 6.39	$....
500	31.92	24.80
1,000	63.85	49.60

Look at the interest one pays. If he borrows $1,000 and makes 24 monthly payments, he pays 24 × $49.60 or $1,190.40. He pays over $190 interest on a $1,000 loan, or an interest rate of about ten and one-half per cent. (The true interest rate would actually be higher because the borrower does not have the use of the entire $1,000 for the whole 24-month period.) And this does not include the customary service charges!

To illustrate what could be involved when a family repeatedly makes small loans, let us take an extreme example. A family wants to buy a washer and drier costing $400. A small loan of $500 is negotiated and the washer and drier is purchased. The other $100 is used for miscellaneous purposes. In a few months, the loan is paid down to $400. The borrower is reminded that he can refinance back to $500 and thus secure another $100. So the family borrows the $100 for miscellaneous needs. This family becomes so intrigued with the fact that additional ready cash is available as soon as the principal is reduced a few dollars that refinancing becomes a habit. The loan is never paid off below $400. What does this mean? It means that the family actually never pays for the washer and drier. After the appliances are worn out, the family is still paying interest on the $400, to say nothing of the service charge that recurs each time the loan is refinanced. It does not take long to pay out as much in interest and service charges as the original cost of the appliances. And what does this family realize from such entangling financial manipulations? Simply an extra $50 or $100 every few months to spend here and there. There is no long range lifting of the family's living standard. And the sad factor is that families least able to afford it are the ones so often beguiled into riding these endless merry-go-rounds.

There are times when it is sound practice to borrow. Major purchases and unforeseen emergencies must rely on loans. But it is unsound to build the entire family budget on a dollar down and a dollar-from-here-on-out basis.

Some skill and a great deal of experience will be needed in deciding what amounts to allow for various items in the budget. This will depend on such factors as the amount of income, local living costs, etc. The good steward will recognize that many of the basic necessities of life can be provided at relatively modest cost. Take clothing, for example. A family can be sensibly clothed at reasonable costs, or price can be forgotten in a mad rush to copy the latest fashion magazines. The well-dressed person is not necessarily the man with a dozen pairs of shoes and ten suits, but the man who exercises sound judgment in selecting quality merchandise. It would be better, e.g., to have one or two good basic outfits which one wears day after day than a closet full of cheap, gaudy clothing or excesses of the latest fashions which one cannot afford.

The same is true with food. Expensive food is not necessarily the most nutritious. The National Research Council's Food and Nutrition Board points out, e.g., that a 1½ cup serving of raw cabbage @ 4 cents gives as much Vitamin C as 3¼ cups canned pineapple juice costing 27 cents. One-fourth cup of carrots @ 2 cents provides the minimum daily adult requirement of Vitamin A, the same as 2½ cups of fresh asparagus @ 48 cents. And 1½ cups of cooked dry beans costing only 4 cents provides the same protein as 3½ ounces of ham costing 33 cents! *

Today's shopper does little detailed planning at home. She makes an average of fourteen purchases each trip to the supermarket. She

* Prices will vary locally. Comparative cost is the point. Statistics suggested by U. S. Department of Agriculture.

plans to buy four of these items. Ten are selected on impulse. And of the ten, seven are items she never dreamed of buying when she left home! Impulse buying is more likely to be in favor of higher profit-margin products, such as speciality and gourmet foods. Careful budgeting, with preplanned purchases, will enable a family to meet its basic nutrition needs economically.

This is not to suggest that a wife must serve beans seven nights a week to be a good steward! It is saying that common sense, foresight, and prudence will enable a family to do far more with its money than the family which exercises little judgment in its spending, giving way entirely to the subtleties of the 1,518 advertising media that greet the average family in a fifteen-hour day!

These pointers should not imply that a good steward is a basement-bargain chaser. Nor are they to insinuate that frugality is synonymous with stewardship, that credit is evil, or that slavish adherence to a budget is spirituality.

The purpose is to magnify the fact that good stewardship includes the total management of one's material possessions, and that intelligence, foresight, and common sense are in no way foreign to Christian stewardship.

Are you satisfied with the stewardship of your spending habits? If so, you are ready for the sixth and final step, "How will I leave my money?"

CHAPTER SEVEN

HOW WILL I LEAVE MY MONEY?

There are a number of us, who creep
Into the world to eat and sleep
 And know no reason why we are born
 Save only to consume the corn,
Devour the cattle, flock and fish
And leave behind an empty dish.

ANONYMOUS

"But pastor, you can see the reason why we are not for this new educational building. We are not going to be around too much longer to enjoy the building, and we do not feel like putting money into it." So apologized a group of older members for not endorsing a building program in their church.

We are not going to be here to enjoy it! Is Christianity just something to enjoy? Or is it primarily an opportunity for service with happiness as a by-product? Does the Great Commission apply only during one's lifetime? What about the twenty centuries in which the saints of God pressed the battle against the gates of hell before we were born? Or the ten or twenty or thirty centuries they will continue the battle after we are gone? Will we have less interest in the Lord's work from the bleachers of heaven—or merely day-dream eternity away on some nebulous "Beautiful Isle of Somewhere"?

This poses step six in the stewardship of material possessions: "How will I leave my money when I die?"

94

One is not the steward he ought to be until he spells out how his money is to be used after his death. There is a continuing responsibility for material wealth that outlives one's physical body. To earn honestly, view sacredly, give liberally, and spend wisely is not enough. The final test of the worthy steward is the disposition of his money at his death. This is his last opportunity to show the sincerity of his Christian profession. If he intentionally or unintentionally omits God from his last will and testament then he has said, "My interest in the Lord's work is limited to my lifetime and the benefits it will bring to me." But in a Christian will he says, "God's kingdom is forever. I have played my little part during my lifetime. Now I verify my interest in its continuing prosperity by leaving a portion of my estate for its support."

Everyone Leaves Something

Inevitably when a wealthy person dies, someone asks, "How much did he leave?" And the answer is always the same, "He left it all!" This is true alike of the wealthy and the poor. All leave something, and all leave all of that something. No man is so poor but that he leaves some estate, and no man is so privileged and wealthy that he is allowed to take even one crumb when he crosses Jordan. "For we brought nothing into this world, and it is certain we can carry nothing out" (1 Tim. 6:7).

Although the material wealth one leaves is important, there are other legacies even more vital. William S. Marquis wrote in his will:

I desire to bequeath to my children and their families, my testimony to the truth and preciousness of the Gospel of Jesus Christ. This heritage of Christian faith, received in an unbroken line from exiled and persecuted Huguenot and Scots Covenanter ancestors, is of infinitely more value than any houses, lands or bonds. . . . As life's sun sinks toward its setting I want to say to my dear children and grandchildren in this private document: "Hold fast to the faith and fellowship and service of Jesus Christ and his Church." They will make life worth living under any conditions.

And Patrick Henry wrote:

I have now disposed of all my property to my family. There is one thing more I wish I could give them, and that is the Christian religion. If they had that, and I had not given them one shilling, they would have been rich; and if they had not that, and I had given them all the world, they would be poor.

To leave behind what we own is to suggest the incompleteness of life. Unspent money means a portion of life unlived that may have been anticipated. Nor is unspent money all that is left. G. K. Chesterton said of Robert Louis Stevenson, "He died with a thousand stories in his heart." When Raphael was buried, his last picture—only half complete—was borne in the funeral procession. The last sentence in Sir Walter Scott's journal broke off suddenly, "Tomorrow we shall . . ." And Franz Schubert left his great "Unfinished Symphony."

Because human life always seems so fragmentary, incomplete, and unfinished, there is the universal longing that it shall be completed. The Christian finds this hope fulfilled in the eternal life promised to all believers.

But the Christian goes a step further. Not only does he anticipate eternal life for himself beyond the grave, but he seeks a way to complete the unfinished task he began in this life. He trusts this task will be fulfilled through his Christian influence that lives on in the lives of his children and friends. He also sees a Christian will as an opportunity to continue the work of Christ in which he has shared in a personal way during his lifetime.

The sincere steward cannot win to Christ all he would like to in his life. He cannot help support all the missionaries, or print all the literature he desires. But after his death, his money can keep busy printing Bibles, building churches, winning the lost. There are a thousand unfinished stories of the triumph of the gospel which he can help write through the estate he leaves, all of which means every Christian steward wants to write the will of God in his will.

He sees a Christian will as a way of depositing deathless dollars in the vaults of eternity. He senses that the Christian owes—but does not own—what he possesses.

There was a day when it was thought estate planning was only for the wealthy. Today this is the privilege of every man. And, in a Christian will, it is not so much the amount one leaves as it is the testimony it gives. Even a very small estate that remembers the cause of Christ unmistakably says, "Here is a man that cared—even after he was gone."

Fortunately, state laws give an individual the right to decide how his money is to be spent after his decease. But this decision must be made—and in writing—while one is living. The property of one who dies intestate (without a will) will be distributed according to the laws of the state, which may or may not be in harmony with the desires of the deceased. Sentiment, emotion, intentions—all are set aside for the rigid requirements of law when one fails to leave a will.

A radiant lady in her seventies, still active as a teacher and visitor in her church, joyously described the will she and her husband signed before his death. "My greatest satisfaction is knowing that my will is in Dr. Cauthen's * desk. At my death, what little I own will go to the Lord's work." Is it any wonder she was active and happy at an age when some spend most of their time in self-pity? For her, life was not to end the day her name appeared in an obituary column. Life was to continue, and her money was to continue in usefulness in the manner *she had decided.*

Practical Suggestions

In following any suggestions regarding estate planning, remember that there is no substitute for competent legal help. Such advice is worth more than it costs. Remember also that laws vary from state to state. The helps given herewith are general and suggestive only. Do not rely on them for specific help.

Consider the wisdom of distributing your estate preceding your death, i.e., actually dispose of your wealth under your personal supervision. Sir Francis Bacon said, "Defer not charities till death; for, certainly if a man weighs it rightly, he that doth so is rather liberal of another man's than his own." This would be inadvisable for a younger person (unless he were of substantial worth). But the life annuity (described below) is a method that allows the

* Executive Secretary of the Southern Baptist Foreign Mission Board

donor to transfer his assets to a given institution before his death and receive a stipulated income as long as he lives.

The value in disposing of one's material wealth before death is in the satisfaction one receives from knowing his money has gone to the object intended. In *The Grace of Giving*, P. E. Burroughs describes an outright gift of $100,000 received by a divinity school from an aging couple. At first they had wished to remember the school in their will. But a school official advised, "Please don't do that. I appreciate your thought, but you must know that not more than fifty per cent of the amount named in wills for institutions ever gets to them. Distant relatives may enter plea and disturb the most carefully-written will. If you wish to do something for us, make an outright gift."

Avoid freak wills or wills that could tie up trust funds in perpetuity because of fantastic stipulations. One eccentric woman is reported to have left a million dollars for a dog hospital. Over the door was to be inscribed, "The more I saw of people, the more I thought of dogs." During the days of the California gold rush, a St. Louis mayor left his money in trust to aid pioneers whose wagons broke down or whose bacon gave out! Covered wagons were long extinct before the funds were exhausted. Yet the donor had so restricted the use of his estate that it could be used for no other purpose.

A will should be made when one is young and in good health. As one's status changes, the will can be altered from time to time. But death-bed wills are the most easily broken, and are void in some states. If a charitable or religious institution is named in a will, some states require the will to be in force from thirty to ninety days before the testator's death. Some individuals are superstitious about making a will, thinking it forebodes death or old age. Nothing could be farther from the truth. The disposition of one's property following his death is not a decision for aged, sick persons. It requires the best thinking and planning of one who is vigorous, robust, and in full command of his faculties. Remember, when you *need* a will, it is too late to make one!

Seek competent, intelligent legal advice when drawing up a will or making any changes. A will should be signed in the presence of two or more persons not interested in the estate. The witnesses will also sign the will, each in the presence of the other, verifying the authenticity of the signature of the testator.

Name an executor or executrix. If this is omitted, the state will name one at additional expense.

Avoid elaborate, detailed wills with numerous qualifications and exceptions. Simplicity, clarity, and directness are desired. Attach as few strings as possible. A percentage division of an estate is often far better than a dollar division. No one can foretell the exact number of dollars that will eventually be left in the residue of an estate. But whatever is left can always be divided percentage-wise.

Provide specifically for the wife and all of the children. A wife is entitled to a certain share, even though she should be omitted from the will. If a child is to be disinherited or to receive less than his legal share, such should be specifically mentioned. Omitting a child's name will not prevent his sharing in the estate. A couple may make a joint will, or the husband and wife may write separate wills. Give mention, at least, to every possible dependent so no one could claim he was forgotten.

Estate laws vary from state to state. As one changes his place of residence, employment, or ownership of property, the will should be reviewed and brought into line with existing laws. Subsequent marriage of a testator requires a new will in some states.

Include the will of God. Margaret T. Applegarth succinctly writes, "It takes a lawyer, in the end, to phrase it legally; but it takes a Redeemer to plan it regally—immortal tidings in your mortal hands." [1] In addition to service rendered, savings up to 77 per cent in estate and inheritance taxes are saved through bequests to religious institutions.

Provide a safe place for keeping the will, and file one copy with the chief beneficiary.

Where and How

The Christian steward's first and rightful consideration will be for his dependents. The amount to be left to one's heirs will vary with age, health, and ability to provide for themselves. One would have greater responsibility, e.g., for smaller children than for mature children established in life. A handicapped child would need more than one physically and mentally capable.

One should exercise prudence and common sense in the amount bequeathed to dependents. Harm as well as good can result. Sir Francis Bacon said, "A great estate left to an heir is as a lure to all birds of prey." And Roger W. Babson writes, "We are striving and even slaving to lay up property for our children, when statistics clearly show that the more we lay up for them, the worse off they are going to be. If statistics demonstrate any one thing, they demonstrate that the less money we leave our children, the better off they will be." Individual circumstances will alter each case.

Our primary consideration here is for that portion one invests in Christian causes after caring for his family. The older and fewer one's dependents, the larger this portion will be. One should imitate the spirit of the dying man who was asked where his will could be found. He answered simply, "In the pocket of God!"

What is the advisability of leaving funds to one's church? Perhaps, if outright grants are made whereby the congregation can use the money immediately for such items as new buildings, enlargement of staff, etc. No, if permanent endowment is set up for operating expenses. The latter is discouraged because one of the services rendered by a church is teaching its members to give. If the needs of the church are taken care of, then the church's stewardship message will necessarily be weakened. "Endowed cats catch no mice."

But Christian institutions such as mission boards, colleges or seminaries, homes for dependent children, unmarried mothers, or the aged, hospitals, and so on, are different. The risk of weakening their effectiveness through trust and endowment funds is not nearly so great as in individual churches. Many of them, to operate on sound principles and to render increasing services, must have support of this type.

Methods for distributing wealth or property to Christian institutions are numerous. Most institutions will accept funds, however, through any legitimate arrangement stipulated by the donor.

To simplify giving to religious institutions, many denominations have incorporated non-profit foundations. There are also numerous private foundations of similar nature. These foundations counsel would-be donors, assist in estate planning, serve as administrators, and receive funds which they invest and channel to the institution designated by the donor. Gifts are made *through* but not *to* these foundations.

Twenty-four of the state Baptist conventions affiliated with the Southern Baptist Convention have such foundations, commonly designated as The Baptist Foundation of Alabama, or Georgia Baptist Foundation, or Missouri Baptist Foundation, etc. The Southern Baptist Foundation is a convention-wide foundation, sponsored by the Southern Baptist Convention.

Typical of these foundations is this statement of purpose by the Louisiana Baptist Foundation:

The Louisiana Baptist Foundation is an agency of the Louisiana Baptist Convention, a corporation chartered under the laws of our state. It purposes to provide information about needs of Baptist institutions and causes and to serve individuals in the Christian stewardship planning of their possessions. It is charged with administering trust funds placed with it for safekeeping and investment.

The operating budget of the Foundation comes entirely from the Cooperative Program, thus making it possible for the Foundation to devote its time and energies to others. It does not exist for itself. It lives to serve.

There are at least five advantages in using the services of one of these foundations:

Advice of a general nature is available, free without obligation. Customarily, a foundation will provide legal help by a competent attorney in drawing up a will or planning an estate.

A foundation will serve as administrator for an estate, again without cost if certain qualifications are met.

Since the foundations are nonprofit, bequests to them frequently enjoy liberal tax-free benefits. Savings are available on such taxes as inheritance, estate, income, and capital gains.

Administrative and operating costs of the foundations are commonly provided from Cooperative Program receipts. Thus, the donor has the satisfaction of knowing that all of his bequest is going directly to the cause named, with no "handling" or service charges.

The foundations have pertinent information on the needs and opportunities of all Baptist boards and institutions, enabling the donor to gain a wide perspective of possible beneficiaries before deciding on a beneficiary. Donors should always be careful of favoring the needs which are apparent and close at home without a fair consideration of total world opportunities.

Methods of transferring money or property to a foundation are flexible, and the donor enjoys great liberty at this point. Here are five broad patterns for estate planning. This is not an exclusive listing, and there are variations within each plan:

Gift annuities.—These are also known as living trusts, life trusts, life annuities, and living endowments. Such gifts are made before the death of the donor, and are becoming an increasingly popular means to dispose of one's wealth preceding death, yet maintain a life income. The donor gives property to the foundation in any form, such as real estate, cash, stocks, bonds, etc. The foundation receives the bequest and invests it for the annuitant, giving him a guaranteed income for as long as he lives. The annuity received by the donor depends on his age when the bequest is made. A donor under thirty commonly receives a 3 per cent return, while donors in their seventies receive up to 6 per cent and more. A joint annuity may be set up whereby, e.g., a husband and wife both share in the income for as long as either shall live.

There are good reasons for the growing popularity of this plan. First, tax benefits. The initial bequest is tax-deductible as a gift to a religious organization, and the income is largely free from income tax. Second, a gift annuity, unlike other forms of investment, does not require reinvestment every few years. Unlike other securities, there is positively no fluctuation in value or dividends. The rate of an annuity, once established, never changes, regardless of war or business conditions. Third, the testator becomes the executor of his own will, placing his money in his own lifetime just where he wants it to go. All the expenses and unpleasantness associated so frequently with the settlement of wills are avoided. There are no executor commissions, court or counsel charges, or inheritance taxes.

At the death of the annuitant, the principal goes to the institution named by the annuitant.

Outright gifts of cash or other securities.—These may be given before death, or stipulated in a will. The donor may name the institution to be favored, and indicate if the principle is to be used, or whether only the interest is to be utilized, with the principle permanently invested.

Endowment funds.—This is a permanent fund set aside for a specific use, with the income applied perpetually for the purposes stipulated. The donor may endow, e.g., a teaching chair in some college or seminary, a scholarship or loan fund, or some phase of the operative expenses of an institution. Funds given through outright grants, annuities, or wills may be so designated for endowment purposes.

Memorial funds.—Again, the necessary money or property may be granted in an outright gift, annuity, or a will. The benefiting cause is chosen at the discretion of the giver. Either the donor, or a relative, or some other person he designates may be memorialized by having his name affixed in some manner to the fund.

Life insurance.—The foundation or institution is named as a beneficiary, and at the donor's death the insurance company pays the proceeds directly, with no need for an executor or court fees. A will affects in no way the provisions of an insurance policy. Proceeds from the policy may be used for endowment, memorial fund, or any other purpose designated by the donor.

The various state and convention foundations (Baptist) are anxious to answer any calls for information or counsel. Free literature is available upon request, as well as personal counsel.

Other denominations render similar services. The Presbyterian Church, U. S., promotes legacies and bequests through The Presbyterian Foundation, Inc., with offices in Charlotte, North Carolina. This Foundation distributes promotional literature and counsels with prospective donors who wish to remember Presbyterian causes. Each of the four major Presbyterian boards, as well as Presbyterian institutions, also distribute literature and provide legal counsel and other help for those who are interested. Their Board of World Missions receives the major share of Presbyterian bequests.

The Methodist Church encourages each of its local congregations to organize a Committee on Wills and Legacies. This Committee, authorized by the Discipline of the Methodist Church, encourages each member to continue his stewardship through the drawing up of a Christian will. In addition, Conference committees hold district workshops and consultations on estate planning. Promotional materials are distributed through a Committee on Wills, Bequests and Gifts of the Council on World Service and Finance at 740 Rush Street, Chicago 11, Illinois. Included is a "Wills and Legacies Newsletter" sent six times a year to pastors and local church chairmen.

A Methodist layman from Wisconsin writes, "Albert Einstein said, 'I remind myself that my inner and outer life depends on the labor of other men, living and dead. I must exert myself to give in the same manner I have received and am receiving.' We can well take these words to heart. The world must not be poorer because we were here. Our work for God must not cease when we depart. We must leave something that will carry on."

The Stewardship of Influence

It is not enough for the careful steward to dispose of his surplus wealth according to Christian principles. He should use his influence to persuade other Christians to do likewise.

Testimonies on the blessings of tithing are frequently given in worship services and Sunday school assemblies. Why not enlist laymen who have made Christian wills (or other disposition of their property through life annuities, etc.) to bring occasional testimonies on the blessing this has been to them?

Some churches have considered the possibility of printing a request for information on the back of their annual pledge cards.

Appropriate space would be given for members to check whether or not they have made a will, and whether they would like to have free counsel regarding estate planning without obligating themselves. Granted only a few signed this part of the card in any given year, the procedure would give opportunity for annual promotion of estate planning.

The pastor and other staff members have unusual opportunities for encouraging Christian estate planning. Dr. J. W. Storer, executive secretary of the Southern Baptist Foundation, writes out of personal experience:

In forty-four years of service as a pastor, I thought that I had covered the waterfront—that I had majored on the great fundamentals, fed the flock, instructed in those things which made for the development of the people into well grounded and rounded stewards. . . .

But it has dawned on me since coming to my present position that I have failed miserably to lead my people into the consideration of one of the most vital things of life. . . .

How did it occur that I who preached so much about the resurrection . . . overlooked so much the investment of life after death? . . . But if it were to do over again there would be prominent space given in my sermon scheduling, in the midweek service, and in the study courses for this immortal business of stewardship of money after death.[2]

The Tennessee Baptist Foundation suggests seven ways pastors can encourage Christian estate planning:

Familiarize themselves with the various state and convention foundations and the agencies and institutions they serve.

Enclose tracts in letters, use bulletin boards, and utilize sermons, midweek services, and study courses.

Set the example of planning their own estates and giving some publicity to it in a manner that will render service without being offensive.

Furnish names of prospective donors to the state and Convention foundations.

Arrange for conferences between local persons and foundation officials.

Emphasize the work of the foundations during September, the

month on the denominational calendar set aside for foundation promotion.

Emphasize "Write your will" each January, utilizing the denominational literature available each year on this theme.

Ways to Live Longer

Anyone is assured of an immediate fortune who can devise a method to prolong human life. The desire to live is inherent in every person. Time passes too quickly.

> When, as a child, I laughed and wept,
> Time crept.
> When, as a youth, I dreamed and talked,
> Time walked.
> When I became a full grown man,
> Time ran.
> And later, as I older grew,
> Time flew.
> Soon I shall find, while travelling on,
> Time gone.[3]

Careful estate planning is one way for the Christian steward to live longer. The money he accumulates in life can be disciplined and channeled to work for him and for Christ's cause long after death has claimed his body and heaven has called for his soul.

And let emphasis be placed on careful planning. One who wisely and thoughtfully plans his estate can joyfully anticipate the good that will continue beyond his death. The good that results will not be a happen-so, but will have the same explanation given by a colored servant for the large number of flowers at the funeral of his employer. In answer to a bystander who commented on the unusual floral arrangements, the servant answered simply, "Yassuh, but you know, he been planting the seeds for them flowers a long time!"

Ordinarily, the man who has cared little for Christ in life will care little for his cause in death. This inscription, which appears on a headstone in the small churchyard at Leamington, England, could well be inscribed on many today:

> Here lies a miser who lived for himself,
> And cared for nothing but gathering pelf,
> Now, where he is, or how he fares,
> Nobody knows and nobody cares.

Compare this with the testimony of a Baptist layman who said, "My wife and I have recently reached a decision. Through all these years, we have given the Lord a tenth. Surely we can do that much after we are gone, and we have so provided in our will." Interests in the sunset of life normally follow the interests of the noonday of life.

A good steward plans a Christian estate as proof of his continuing interest in the worthwhile things of life. There is the longing in the breast of every Christian for the significant, the meaningful in life, as expressed in this beautiful prayer:

Eternal God, tie me to something eternal. I tie myself to things—houses, lands—but some twist of fate robs me of them. I tie myself to love, but one microbe takes my loved one out of my life forever. I tie myself to a friend who ceases to understand me. Tie thou me to truth, ageless like thyself. Tie thou me to a purpose, endless like thyself. Tie thou me to work, the lifelong savior of hands and heart and brain . . . Tie thou me to human need, for thereby thou hast redeemed many. Tie thou me to Christ, who said, "Abide in me." Tie thou me to thyself, who failest not.[4]

This longing can find partial fulfilment in a final Christian disposition of property. An example is found in the will of Benjamin Franklin, who left a sum of money for a public library in Philadelphia. The investment continues to bear fruit to this day. Its value was made clearer a few years ago when a group of laborers doing some excavation work in Philadelphia unearthed a can containing some old coins and bank notes. The paper money was rotten and useless, but the men quickly grabbed up the coins and used them for a few drinks. Examination showed that the original value of the buried money equaled that left by Benjamin Franklin. The only difference was the good accomplished. The former brought enlightenment to young minds, the latter bought a few beers at a corner saloon.

Harry Lauder, the Scottish comedian, liked to describe the old lamplighter who came by his boyhood home each evening to light the gas lamps. He would light the lamp in front of Lauder's home, then make his way, back and forth, down the street. In the deepening twilight, the lad would lose sight of the old lamplighter. "But," he explained, "I always knew where he was by the avenue of light he left behind him."

The train of light he left behind! Here is a parable of life. We make our way down the avenue of life, first on one side, then on the other side of the street. Sometimes we run, again we walk. Occasionally we stop to rest. But evening comes and twilight wraps its purple mantle around our shoulders. Then it is dark. But our friends, our loved ones, have an unmistakable indication of where we are going by the light we leave behind. The wise use of money, in life and in death, is but one of many ways of letting our light shine.

Perhaps that is what Robert Wild had in mind when he wrote:

An Epitaph

for ye godly man's tomb

Here lies a piece of Christ; a star in dust; a vein of gold; a china dish that must be used in heaven, when God shall feast the just.

Twilight, and night, and death—for the Christian they are not the ending but the beginning. They mark the entrance into the fuller stewardship of eternity. They signal the commendation of the Master Steward, "Well done, thou good and faithful servant: thou hast been faithful over a few things, I will make thee ruler over many things: enter thou into the joy of thy lord" (Matt. 25:21). The "few things" include, among others, the six steps in the stewardship of material possessions: how money is earned, how it is viewed, why it is given, how it is given, how it is spent, and how it is left.

Is it too much for the faithful steward to hope that at his home-going it may be said as it was of Mr. Valiant for Truth,

". . . and all the trumpets sounded!"

CHAPTER EIGHT
THE SIX STEPS IN CHURCH FINANCE

"Now concerning the collection . . . "
(*1 Cor. 16:1*).

Will those of you who have been putting buttons in the collection basket, kindly put in your own buttons, and not those from the church upholstery.[1]

"If you would like to make a donation to our new building, raise your hand and one of our ushers will give you an envelope!"

"Now folks, we're behind with last month's bills, but we can catch up if everyone will chip in a little heavier today!"

"Remember our annual church picnic this Friday. We need several more cakes, pies, and homemade candy."

"All of us have friends who will buy some chances on the new Buick. This is a good cause, and someone is going to win a new car by helping our church."

Is it any wonder that many ask, "Why are the churches always asking for money?" Some feel that stewardship is simply passing the offering plate during a Sunday morning interlude of organ music. Still others picture the church as a street-corner beggar holding out a hat full of pencils; or, others think of the church as a savings account, whose chief end is to show a larger balance at the end of each month than the preceding month.

Churches have an opportunity to dignify the doctrine of steward-ship with a well organized, scriptural plan of church finance. Or they can cheapen and weaken the doctrine by haphazard, spas-modic methods of receiving and disbursing funds.

A good system of church finance will aid the individual members primarily with step four, "How Do I Give My Money?" Attention will be given in this chapter to practical suggestions for an effective pattern of church finance that will strengthen this step. But while the churches utilize these suggestions, they will be careful in their preaching and educational ministries to help their members at the point of earning, viewing, spending, and leaving money as well as help in giving it properly.

There are few areas in the Christian life at which the churches can render more lasting benefit to their members than in the area of stewardship. Lives and families will be blessed, churches strengthened, and new joy found in Christian service when well-planned stewardship programs are adopted.

A Mission to Perform

One of the first services a church should render its members is showing them that although a church is not a business, it has busi-ness to perform. As such, money is needed to carry out its func-tions. Money will not solve all problems, but it will help. Conse-quently, a church should be unafraid to ask its members for money, and lots of it. No apology should be made in discussing church finance. It is just as scriptural, just as Christian, and just as proper as talking about loving one's neighbor or attending church on Sun-day. Henry B. Trimble notes:

The Church has been too long apologetic about asking that its peo-ple be generous. Is the Church asking for money? Certainly it is; and it will always be asking for money so long as there is human need, and the Spirit of Christ lives in the Church. Religion is not an easy convenience. It is life's greatest challenge, both in the sense of the magnitude of its program, and also in the call to sacrifice that it makes to all disciples. The Church offers no easy way, nor can it do so. It is an institution of martyrs and heroes. Most of the men who wrote the New Testament, or dared to follow Christ in the first century, finally wore the martyr's crown. When we as Christians try to live a life of ease, without sacrifice for the cause, we are attempting to unite incompatibles.[2]

Ways and Means

Possible error and harm lie in *how* the churches ask for money, and not in the fact of asking. In the main, churches have historically followed four methods of asking for funds.

Taxation.—For centuries the state churches in Europe were tax-supported. Nonmembers and unbelievers had the same financial responsibility toward a state church as communicants. The separation of church and state in this country necessitated other methods. This requirement has proved a blessing because it has placed responsibility for church support where it belongs—on the voluntary contribution of voluntary members. There is widespread agreement that church support by taxation is a poor method of teaching the stewardship of material possessions.

Commercialism.—Happily, this is a custom that seems to be on the wane, at least in most non-Catholic churches. But there are always those who feel that an "easy" way for a church to meet its budget is to sponsor a carnival or supper, sell tickets to a play, conduct a bazaar, or even resort to games of chance. Such methods may fatten church treasuries, but they do not grow great stewards. They appeal more to the appetite and selfish interests of the participants than to their spiritual development.

An indictment of commercialism is even more clearly drawn in Moffatt's translation of 2 Corinthians 8:1–4:

Now, brothers, I have to tell you about the grace God has given to the churches of Macedonia. Amid a severe ordeal of trouble, their overflowing joy and their deep poverty together have poured out a flood of rich generosity; I can testify that up to their means, aye and beyond their means, they have given—begging me of their own accord, most urgently, for the favour of contributing to the support of the saints.

Begging.—This is a general reference to any fund-raising effort that places a church in the role of a beggar or panhandler. As long as the general public conceives of a church as an object of charity, worthy of an occasional tip or handout, that church has miserably failed to develop its members in the stewardship of material possessions. Unfortunately, many churches have been satisfied to be labeled as charities, pointing their appeal to the pity and sentiment of the potential giver. Sentimental alms-giving may provide bare subsistence to the street-corner beggar; it will never support the globe-girdling mission of a New Testament church.

Christian stewardship.—This, again, is a very general reference, including all that churches do to link giving and church finance to Christian consecration. Churches that teach Christian stewardship are not raising money to pay bills, or simply enlisting tithers, but they are guiding their members into a higher plane of living that includes the total man and his life responsibilities, one by-product of which is ample funds to carry out the work of the church.

Fallacies in Church Finance

Before proceeding with practical suggestions for a well-rounded church finance program, certain fallacies or misunderstandings should be noted. There are at least six.

The fallacy that the more money people have, the more they give.—It is true that during prosperous years, per capita gifts to churches are higher on a dollar basis, but these gifts are smaller on a proportionate or percentage basis. People give more dollars when they earn more, but they seemingly give a smaller proportion of their total income at such times. Conversely, during times of economic recession, people give a larger percentage of their income for Christian causes.

For example, during the mid-depression year of 1933 Americans gave nearly twice as much, percentage-wise, to religious and benevolent causes as they did during prosperous 1956. Of course they gave more dollars in 1956 than 1933 because there were more dollars to give from. But they gave a smaller slice of each dollar in 1956 than in 1933.

Church leaders should be aware of this common fallacy, for conservative members will use it to discourage any out-reaching and challenging program, except during the most prosperous years. It is strange, but true, that the more one earns, the more he wants to keep for himself. The less one earns, the greater is his willingness to share a larger proportion with others. There is an unusual strain in human nature that leads a man to share his last crust of bread with more readiness than he would a million dollars!

The fallacy that churches are dependent for their support on the well-to-do.—Conservative members sometimes use this fallacy to limit the program of their church by complaining, "But we have no wealth in our church!" So what? Ask any pastor who has seriously studied the average giving records of his church and he will say, "The major support of our church comes from the rank and file member on a weekly income." The secret of church finance is a large number of small but regular givers, rather than the small group of large but perhaps spasmodic contributors.

The fallacy that the more offerings a church takes, the greater will be its income.—Again, experience shows that the average congregation builds up a natural resistance when the offering plate is passed too frequently. "But you can't ask a consecrated Christian to give too much!" True, but you can ask him to give too often! Many churches have found that one well-planned offering a week, in which every member is urged to participate, whether present or absent, is far superior to crying "Wolf! Wolf!" every time a bill comes due, resulting in two or three special offerings every Sunday.

The fallacy that giving is a substitute for service.—"Let the pastor visit—that's what we pay him to do!" But what the pastor does can never substitute for the service expected of the members. It is impossible for one to "pay" another to render service for him. Missionaries are not paid to go overseas for us. Pastors are not paid to pray and witness for us. But missionaries are paid to *assist* us in the world task of evangelism, not to substitute for us. Pastors are paid to *help* us in our mutual task of witnessing, visiting, and teaching.

What Jean Jacques Rousseau wrote about citizenship is true of church membership, "As soon as public service ceases to be the chief business of the citizens, and they would rather serve with their money than with their persons, the State is not far from its fall." [3]

The fallacy that church finance and stewardship are synonymous. —Church finance is one small area of stewardship, and should be so taught in the churches. This fallacy is encouraged by unwitting pastors or teachers who emphasize stewardship *only in connection with a request for funds.* P. E. Burroughs wisely sounds this caution,

> When a minister preaches the tithe for the sake of the budget he has unwittingly cheapened a great message, which may, therefore, be defeated by its own irreverence. . . .
> Mr. Calkins has coined for us a phrase which is worthy of careful thought: "High truth, for revenue, awakens suspicion." What prompts the special emphasis which we put on the tithe? Is it soul-growth that we seek or is it the filling of depleted treasuries? Doubtless we seek both, but which of the two is primary? [4]

The fallacy that if the church gets a man's money, it will invariably get the man.—Jesus did state as a general principle, "For where your treasure is, there will your heart be also" (Matt. 6:21). But Jesus always asked for the man first, and then his money. Remember that one of his severest criticisms was aimed at the Pharisees who excelled in the giving of tithes, but gave every evidence of lack of personal consecration and warmth of spirit. The Jewish religious system had the Pharisees' money; God did not have their lives. And although it is a general truth that heart interests follow dollar interests, it is possible for an individual to give generously of his money and withhold himself. Highly improbable, yes. But possible. And sufficiently possible that church leaders should be alert for this fallacy in their congregations.

An Annual Emphasis

Assuming a church undergirds its entire educational and preaching ministry with basic stewardship teaching that emphasizes the total dedication of life, there is still needed an all-out, annual presentation of the church's financial program and securing of pledges for the same.

Such an annual effort should be just as much a part of the regular program as the vacation Bible school, revivals, teacher training courses, and promotion day. Time will be set aside in the calendar, funds made available, and leadership trained to make this an effective feature each year in the life of the congregation.

Most churches follow the calendar year for their fiscal year, the new budget becoming operative on each January 1. This suggests October and November as budget promotion months. Through the years, a number of churches have devised their own budget campaigns. Techniques and length of time for the campaigns have varied, but ordinarily they included an educational and promotional phase that seeks to reach every member with a stewardship, tithing, and budget message, followed up with a more or less intensive canvass of the members for annual pledges.

Most annual budget programs begin with the preparation of a budget goal, inclusive enough to provide for all causes and large enough to challenge the congregation. One church, faced with the decision of whether to have an annual budget campaign, said, "We do not need such an effort this year. We are already reaching our budget!"

Already reaching the budget? What budget? One that meets ordinary operating expenses? Any church is challenged to place its budget beside the Great Commission and then honestly answer, "Are we meeting the needs?" It is absolutely impossible for a church to receive more money than it can use, providing that church has a missionary and evangelistic spirit. Each church is responsible for taking the gospel to all nations, and if any church is receiving sufficient funds to do so, we have yet to hear of it!

For a church to say that it has no need to challenge its members to give more is to encourage them to give less. To hold back on an annual educational program regarding the financial program of the church is to rob new Christians and growing children of the opportunity to assume their share. The responsibility is inescapable for the church that wishes to provide a balanced ministry.

An annual, repetitive, consistent program will do far more good than the occasional, spasmodic, emotional-type of effort. Sometime ago a finance committee met to find a way to pay overdue church bills. One layman suggested, "I've got it! Let each member of this committee quietly resolve that we will try the tithe for one month. Maybe enough will come in to meet the bills." Several agreed, until another layman spoke up, "Tithing is fine, but I don't believe in playing around with God!" He meant that if tithing were right, it should be practiced consistently and taught as a regular feature of church life. He was discouraging novel ideas designed to "test" or "prove" God. It is doubtful if one should test tithing for a month any more than he would test telling the truth for a month!

The annual budget campaign, starting with a budget goal and culminating with written pledges by all the members, may well follow this simple formula: "Tell everybody, use everybody, see everybody." Or this pattern:

Proposal.—Dreaming, or what we *would* like to do for our church if funds were available.

Appraisal.—What we *could* do if every member were interested in proportion to their ability.

Cultivation.—Publicity, information, fellowship, inspiration.

Visitation.—Footwork and contacts. See and enlist everyone.

The annual budget campaign is worthy of the same intensive prayer, planning, and work that goes into an evangelistic or enlargement effort. Church leaders who fail in this area are neglecting a vital phase of their ministry. Secondary and irrelevent are the matters of whether the bills are being paid, whether the members are "giving all they can," whether the congregation is rich or poor, and whether or not some individual is "agin" it. If the whole gospel is taught and preached, stewardship becomes a requisite and not an elective.

Some churches that resent such an annual effort may be like the old man who complained, "This plan ain't spiritual—I don't like it." And it wasn't, for his only idea of spirituality was hollering his head off each Sunday!

Recently, the Southern Baptist Convention has developed for its churches a package-type campaign that includes complete literature and instructions for a twenty-nine day budget program. Help is given in planning, promoting, and pledging the annual church budget. An organization chart is included, as well as a step-by-step calendar of activities. Known as the Forward Program of Church Finance of Southern Baptists, it is in wide and successful use in many churches. In addition to the basic *Guidebook*, the program offers certain thematic materials in annual editions. Typical annual themes have been "I Will Be Faithful," "Give As God Has Given," "Because God Loved," "Give to Win!", and so on. The annual theme is carried out in the posters, pledge cards, tracts, art work, etc., available. Churches which feel they are not able to employ the full program to pledge their budgets may choose one of three applications, C, B, and A. Thus, a church may step-up in usefulness of the program as it uses more and more features each year. Full information may be secured by writing to SBC Stewardship Services, 127 Ninth Avenue, North, Nashville 3, Tennessee.

A variety of stewardship materials and budget promotion methods is available in the various denominations. For example, the Protestant Episcopal Church produces literature for year-around stewardship teaching, in its broadest sense. Then, an annual kit of materials is available to help each parish conduct its own Every Member Canvass. Every effort is made to overcome any tendency to equate stewardship solely with money given to the church. The material does not emphasize the financial needs of the church as a motive for giving. Materials and other information may be secured by writing to the Department of Promotion, National Council of the Protestant Episcopal Church, 281 Park Avenue South, New York 10, New York.

Also typical of denominations furnishing a packaged plan for the Every Member Canvass type of budget promotion is the Church of the Brethren. Included in their plan is a ten-week calendar of activities, an organizational chart with detailed explanation of workers' duties, and promotional materials and literature. The materials are thematic in nature, with a recent year's theme being "Acknowledge God's Priority." This theme and appropriate art work is featured on letterheads, mailing envelopes, bulletin covers, posters, and tracts. This plan includes a "do-it-yourself" turnover chart for use by canvassers. The basic turnover chart is provided by the denomination, and each church personalizes the charts used by its canvassers, through the use of local photographs and data imprinted thereon. Information and materials may be secured by writing Church of the Brethren, 1451 Dundee Avenue, Elgin, Illinois.

The National Council of Churches maintains liaison with the stewardship programs of many of the denominations in the United States and Canada. For general information on most denominations, write the Department of Stewardship and Benevolence, National Council of the Churches of Christ, 257 Fourth Avenue, New York 10, New York.

Week by Week Emphasis

"There, I'm glad that's done for another year," sighed an exhausted pastor following his annual budget campaign. But was it "done"? Hardly—for the conscientious leader will build a sound church finance program week by week, as well as during the annual effort—just as he seeks to win converts daily as well as during stated revivals. Five practical suggestions are given for a year-around church finance program designed to develop worthy stewards:

Issue envelopes.—Each spring (while prices are lower), order enough individual cartons of envelopes for every church and Sunday school member for the coming year. Order the exact dated type (Sunday, Jan. 24, etc.), and have name of church imprinted. Order enough for anticipated new church and Sunday school members coming in throughout the year. By the first Sunday in December of each year, write the name of every church and Sunday school member on a separate carton or set. (Begin with youngest baby in the nursery. Do not issue "Mr. and Mrs." sets or "Sam Long and family" sets.) Tie the sets in family bundles and display on long tables in a conspicuous place. In pulpit and bulletin announcements throughout December, urge one member from each family to pick up his family's sets. On Monday following the last Sunday in December, mail all unclaimed envelopes.

Throughout the year, set up a routine for distributing envelopes to all new church and Sunday school members. A simple way is to write a letter of welcome to such members on Monday following their enrolment, explaining that it is the custom of the church to furnish sets of envelopes to new members. Later in the week, mail the individual a set, being careful to remove outdated envelopes first. Issue the envelopes, whether the individual agrees to use them or not, or regardless of how irregular in attendance he may be. The presence of the envelope set in the home is a stewardship teaching tool, and worth the few cents' cost if the member never uses a single envelope.

W. L. Howse describes a visit to a church in Santiago, Chile, where Missionary Oleta Snell had improvised envelopes by mimeographing suitable forms. These she cut by hand, folded, and sewed on two sides on a sewing machine to make offering envelopes. She realized the value of personalized giving and was willing to use scrap materials to make it possible (notwithstanding those who do not want their right hand to know what their left hand is doing because their left hand isn't doing anything)!

Encourage make-up offerings.—Churches are losing untold thousands of dollars each week for lack of a simple, effective emphasis on one offering from every member every Sunday whether present or absent. It is entirely possible that many contributors think they are giving far more than they do, and a simple reminder at this point would be helpful. Suggestions in the bulletin near vacation time are always good. Here is one that has been variously used by many churches. This and similar ideas may be effectively used with a little imagination and initiative.

Now it came to pass as summer drew nigh that Mr. Church Member lifted up his eyes to the hills and said, "Lo, the hot days cometh and even now are at hand. Come let us go into the heights where cool breezes refresh us and glorious scenes await."

"Thou speakest wisely," quoth Mrs. Church Member. "Yet three, yea four, things must we do before we go."

"Three things I can think of, but not four," responded Mr. Church Member. "We must arrange for our flowers to be cared for, our chickens fed, and the mail forwarded, but the fourth eludes my mind."

"The fourth is like unto the first three, yet more important than all.

Thou shalt dig into thy purse and pay thy church pledge, that the good name of the church shall be preserved, and that it may be well with thee, for verily I say unto thee, thou hast more now than thou wilt have when thou dost return."

And it came to pass that Mr. Church Member paid his pledge for the summer, and the treasurer rejoiced greatly, saying, "Of a truth there are those who care for the Lord's work." And it was so!

Magnify giving through one's church.—Some feel that as long as their offerings are meeting human needs, then nonchurch benevolent causes are just as worthy, such as Red Cross and Community Chest. It is true these organizations meet human need and should be supported. But these do not substitute for church-giving.

Remember that the ultimate purpose of the gospel is to make believers, not simply fill empty stomachs. The hungry should be fed, but they should be fed in Christ's name. The help given should point them to the Bread of life. The raising of Lazarus in John 11 is a good example. He was raised not simply so he could live longer or to ease the sorrow of his sisters. Jesus said his "sickness was not unto death, but for the glory of God." And his prayer at the tomb pointed out that the miracle was intended to produce belief in Christ as sent from God.

The key word of John's entire Gospel is "believe" and he claims that all that was written was intended to produce belief in Jesus as the Christ.

So all that one does in the Christian life is directed at making believers. For example, here are two homes for unwed mothers. One has a Christian atmosphere. The other, although benevolent in nature, does not produce a definite Christian witness. A girl entering either would receive splendid care. But in the Christian home, there is the possibility of permanent spiritual help that could change the entire direction of her life.

Now if one has a wishy-washy attitude toward his own church and what it teaches, if one thinks "it doesn't matter what a person believes, just so he is sincere," naturally he will scatter his giving here and there as an indication of the shallowness of his convictions.

And this is saying nothing about the well-doer who works himself into an emotional frenzy distributing Christmas baskets to the needy but by the Fourth of July forgets all about them. While he spends the July Fourth week end at the beach, his neighbor, a systematic giver, may be in church, sharing his gifts of leadership and money—week in and week out—for the spiritual as well as the physical healing of the nations!

Handle funds sacredly.—From the time an offering is placed in the basket until the treasurer disburses it in an authorized check, the church should conscientiously handle and administer it.

A counting or teller's committee should open and verify all envelopes. (Not during the worship services, please. And don't push it off on the church staff Monday morning. Rotate the counting committee and include some nominal givers—when they see what others are giving, they may become ashamed and increase their gifts.)

Some control should be exercised over budget expenditures, so that spending will be in line with authorizations. It is not the responsibility of the treasurer to decide which bills should be paid. It is his responsibility to pay all obligations authorized by the church. If there are insufficient funds to meet all obligations, it is the responsibility of the church to provide them—but it is not the privilege of the treasurer to juggle accounts or decide if the church is "able," e.g., to meet its mission obligations this month! The use of purchase orders or requisition slips aid greatly in budget control.

Monthly reports to the congregation on receipts and expenditures should be faithfully prepared. The reports should be as detailed as practical, and any attempt at secrecy should be avoided. Church officials who leave the impression that the fewer questions asked by the congregation the better are defeating their own purpose. Secrecy always breeds suspicion. Every member has a right to know the facts.

The Broadman Church Finance Record System, available at general and religious book stores, offers detailed instructions, record forms, and bookkeeping supplies to church treasurers and financial secretaries.

Mail monthly or quarterly receipts.—Every church member

should receive a written receipt, at least quarterly, showing his giving record for the previous three months.

The reasons for such are numerous. If for some reason one's offerings are not being received by the church, the receipts will reveal the discrepancy. If a member has been negligent or forgetful in giving, the empty spaces on his report will have reminding power. (Members who give nothing should be mailed receipts as well as the regular givers). The receipts are also valuable for income tax purposes. If a taxpayer's return is seriously questioned, the government may require such a receipt from the church *rather than cancelled checks*. The reason is that a person might frequently ask the church office to cash personal checks for him, but still not give the cash in the offering. Yet he would have cancelled checks showing he had "given" to the church regularly!

There is available a variety of receipt forms. One of the best is the individual Record of Contributions (Form 495–21991) available at general and religious book stores. This is a five-part form. One part is mailed to the individual contributor each quarter, while the fifth copy is kept by the church as a permanent record. Matching window envelopes are also available.

Receipts should be mailed not later than ten days following the last Sunday in the quarter. Members are always encouraged to report any errors or to request further information. Some churches enclose a thank-you note or letter. Each year, Southern Baptist Convention Stewardship Services (see above) offers a series of four "Thank You" tract inserts for insertion in the records of contributions. The tracts are written in a warm, personal style, thanking the contributor for his offerings and courteously reminding him to make up any offerings missed. New tracts are produced annually with such titles as "In Appreciation . . . ," "Your Church is Grateful," "They Thank You, Too," and "He Which Soweth Bountifully."

Project a World Outreach

A mother and small daughter passed a beggar on the street. The little girl wanted to give him something, but the mother explained,

"Come along, dear. It isn't any of our business." That night during her bedtime prayers the girl whispered, "And God, please bless that poor man on the corner." Then she added, "But really, it isn't any of our business, is it, Lord?"

A New Testament plan of church finance will invariably emphasize that all of the world is our business—all of its sin and ugliness, all of its disease and suffering, all of its war and greed, all of its beauty and life, all of its love and kindness, all of its ignorance and misunderstanding.

It *is* a congregation's business to pay the preacher, patch the roof, buy Sunday school literature, and pay the utilities. But it is also a congregation's business to help those who cannot be crowded under its own roof. And there are far more on the outside than inside!

This suggests the twofold mission of a church: to worship and to witness. Or stated in the language of Isaiah 54:2, its task is to improve the quality ("strengthen thy stakes") and increase the quantity ("lengthen thy cords"). Someone has said that the minimum equipment for a Christian steward is a pocket New Testament and a small globe. Both can be carried in one's pocket, and anyone who dares to study the two, each in the light of the other, will be impressed with the responsibility of continually lengthening the cords of the church.

It is fairly easy to worship God; it is more costly to witness for God. Many church members, like Simon Peter, are easily converted to the *person* of Christ, but they require a long and painful process to accept the *program* of Christ. They believe he is the Son of God, but hesitate to sacrifice their comforts and overcome their prejudices to make him known to those of every culture, race, and creed. C. D. Clarke senses this difficulty:

Can there ever be a unity of spirit among neighbors in the world when some are willing to eat cake and drink whiskey, while others starve for want of bread and milk; some are clothed in furs, warm woolens and nylons, while others freeze in threadbare cottons and nakedness . . . some call a doctor for the slightest sniffle, while others with advanced diseases die for the want of medicine; some build air-condi-

tioned, plush-seated cathedrals of stone, steel, and marble to praise
their God, while their neighbor Christians meet in drafty, unheated
houses and the heathen perish for lack of knowledge.[5]

Wise church leaders know that the easiest budget to subscribe is
one adopted by a missionary-minded congregation. Once the members gain a world vision, they are much more eager to pledge toward
and give to the budget of their church. They sense then that there
is no limit to the amount of money which their church can use.
They see beyond a mere bill-paying budget and Friday night suppers. They see the lost world mirrored in the offering plate, and
consider their pledge cards and envelopes as vehicles for helping to
transmit the saving gospel to that world. So writes Harry Emerson
Fosdick,

Money is another pair of legs and, lo! it can go where otherwise we
could never go, walking amid the need of China today or ministering
in India and the islands of the sea. Money is another pair of hands and
it can carry burdens that our own fingers cannot touch in our community, our nation, and around the world. Money is another pair of vocal
cords and it can speak where our voice could not be heard, teaching and
preaching where in personal presence we may never go. What a man
does with his money he is in a real sense doing with himself.[6]

Adoption and promotion of the annual budget affords a wonderful opportunity for missionary teaching. As the budget planning
committee recommends a worthy portion to mission causes, as the
congregation studies the relative worth of those causes over against
those close at home, and as the members pledge sacrificially to
support those causes, mission-mindedness becomes the spirit of the
congregation and missionary zeal its passion.

Thus, stewardship and missions walk hand in hand, brothers and
partners in a global ministry of teaching, healing, and preaching.

"But our members know all of this," one pastor protests. "They
know they should give, they know we need money, they know missionary causes need our support." But do they? Or is all this emphasis on a sound church finance program unnecessary in the development of Christian stewards?

If one is tempted to take lightly the stewardship and finance problems of a church, let him consider the testimony of another pastor who asked a member why she sent all her offerings by mail to a radio and television speaker two thousand miles away. Her answer, "But Pastor, he's doing something, and our church isn't!" Her criticism of her church was unfair, for it was and is doing something, both locally and worldwide. But she didn't know it! Why? Because her church had not been able to cross the street and go down the block with its message. But a speaker of national prominence had gotten his message across hundreds of miles. He had tried; evidently the church had not. It took too much for granted.

Has your church gotten across the street with its stewardship and missionary message? Does it plan wisely, both in annual efforts and week by week promotion, to reach the last fringe member with the basic fundamentals of stewardship? Has it taught that how one earns his money, views his money, gives his money, spends his money, and leaves his money are all important?

Blessed is the church leader who can say with that missionary fund-raiser and global strategist of old, "so that from Jerusalem, and round about unto Illyricum, I have fully preached the gospel of Christ" (Rom. 15:19).

NOTES

Chapter 2

1. Henry B. Trimble, *The Christian Motive and Method in Stewardship* (Nashville: Cokesbury Press, 1929), pp. 122–123.

Chapter 4

1. *Selected Poems of John Oxenham*, ed. Charles L. Wallis (New York: Harper & Brothers, 1948), p. 84. Used by permission.

2. Andrew W. Blackwood, Jr., *The Holy Spirit in Your Life* (Grand Rapids: Baker Book House, 1957), pp. 62–63.

3. Ellis Cowling, *Let's Think About Money* (Nashville: Abingdon Press, 1957), p. 50.

Chapter 5

1. S. R. Driver, *International Critical Commentary: Deuteronomy* (New York: Charles Scribner's Sons, 1895), p. 172.

2. Joseph Marcus, "Tithe," *Universal Jewish Encyclopedia*, ed. Isaac Landman (New York: Universal Jewish Encyclopedia Co., Inc., 1943), X, 254.

3. John M. Versteeg, *The Deeper Meaning of Stewardship* (New York: Abingdon Press, 1923), p. 64.

4. Frank Leavell, *Training in Stewardship* (Nashville: Sunday School Board of the Southern Baptist Convention, 1920), pp. 79, 81.

5. Frank K. Means, *Give Ye* (Nashville: Broadman Press, 1944), p. 23.

6. Peter E. Long, "Top Priority." Used by permission.

Chapter 6

1. Mildred R. Bensmiller, *Christianity Today*, June 6, 1960, p. 13.

2. Arthur Guiterman, *The Speaker*, ed. Paul M. Pearson (New York: Noble & Noble Pub., Inc.), VII, 120.

3. Guy L. Morrill, *Laughing Stewardship Through* (New York: Richard R. Smith & Co., 1931), p. 45.

4. Edwin A. Robinson, *Collected Poems* (New York: The Macmillan Co.).

5. Morrill, *op. cit.*, p. 108.

6. *Ibid.*, p. 19.

7. "To E. L., on His Travels in Greece," *Tennyson's Poetical Works* (Cambridge ed.; Boston: Houghton Mifflin Co.), p. 114.

8. "Life in These United States," *Reader's Digest*, September, 1953, p. 34.

9. Cowling, *op. cit.*, p. 23.

Chapter 7

1. Margaret Applegarth, *Twelve Baskets Full* (New York: Harper & Brothers, 1957), p. 72.

2. J. W. Storer, "It Never Dawned On Me," *Baptist Program* (Nashville), April, 1957, p. 11.

3. Said to be an inscription on the door of a grandfather clock in Chester Cathedral.

4. P. R. Hayward, *Young People's Prayers* (New York: Association Press, 1945), p. 18.

Chapter 8

1. Notice in a Presbyterian church in Scotland.

2. Trimble, *op. cit.*, pp. 170–171.

3. Means, *op. cit.*, p. 199.

4. P. E. Burroughs, *The Grace of Giving* (Nashville: The Sunday School Board of the Southern Baptist Convention, 1934), p. 59.

5. C. D. Clarke, "Committed to Action," *The Commission* (Richmond, Virginia: Foreign Mission Board of the Southern Baptist Convention), p. 4.

6. Julius King, ed., *Successful Fund-Raising Sermons* (New York: Funk & Wagnalls Co., 1953), p. 50.